Feminizing the West

Feminizing the West

Neo-Islam's Concepts of Renewal, War and the State

Revised Edition

MUHAMMED AL DA'MI

authorHOUSE®

AuthorHouse™
1663 Liberty Drive
Bloomington, IN 47403
www.authorhouse.com
Phone: 1-800-839-8640

Published by AuthorHouse   11/13/2014

ISBN: 978-1-4918-6522-4 (sc)
ISBN: 978-1-4918-6523-1 (e)

For Liqa' Al Ward,

Love, wife & never ending support

Contents

Preface

As Muslims, orthodox and nominal, deny the currently common notion that Islam adopts violence and, therefore, justifies terror as a *modus operandi*, one is bound to believe that there is something out of joint among Muslims and non-Muslims that has produced the above notion. There are varying perceptions of the faith, its original tenets and future course. The absence of a uniform perception of this religion may be blamed on the inaccurate approach a majority of Muslims adopt to their religion because they mistake it for history. Once turned into history, religion becomes a record of past events merely, something between a chronicle and a narrative. No less alarming is the vulnerability of history to varying interpretations that may come out with totally dissimilar, if not opposing, conclusions and perceptions concerning the spiritual faith which was already tampered with by the various historians and the successive generations of the turbaned, self-appointed custodians of religion, the so-called *'ulama'*. Among today's exceedingly obsessive phenomena which arose from turning religion into mere history is the development and rapid growth of a politicized and radicalized perception of Islam which deviates from the norm of the original and formal religion at a sharp angle. By the formal and original Islam is meant the spiritual faith of the God-fearing mosque-goers who conceive Islam as a matter of spiritual devotion and of virtuous vs. evil deeds, in line with the conceptions the adherents of other religions maintain. The unbridgeable gap between the religious perception of the mosque-goers and that of the proponents of the politicized and radicalized Islam implies the adequacy of my hypothesis concerning the flaw which arises from reading and seeking a spiritual faith in history, and from the opposing perspectives which are usually loaded by preconceptions and stereotypes, let alone the impact of the legends that were spawned and annexed in the course of time. No less damaging are the elective methods of history-reading and history-presentation in accordance with the timely and transitory purposes which are inspired by the readers' visions of how Islam should be and how should it be presented to the upcoming generations in such a way as to suit premeditated purposes and biased interests. As such, inherent educational habits force their way into the religious lesson, fueled by diverse cultural and sub-cultural paradigms consisting, once again, of more stereotypes and misrepresentations which lead to the chaos of the already perplexing mixture of history and religion that was twisted and channeled into political programs meant to serve societal future visions, accordingly.

I, therefore, argue that an attempt to re-read Islamic history, not as religion as has been done so far, with a fresh perspective, that of the currently pressing status quo, and with a specific reference to terror, may purify the odd mixture of politicized history and politicized religion from the habitual abuse in order to employ them pragmatically and in a focused way to illuminate a certain polemic that was continually operative and decisive in twisting the spiritual faith to by-produce several accretions, including what I am terming 'neo-Islam' throughout the chapters of this volume. Among the purposes of this endeavor is to find out where from the problem of the incongruent interpretations originate and how elective historicism contribute to the making and the growth of a medievalist vision, an ancestral dream, which produced the various forms of neo-Islam, including the political, the fundamentalist and, regrettably, the 'terrorist', if such terms are permissible in the context of the following pages. The chapters that follow are designed to verify that the variants of neo-Islam, irrespective of denominations, are not Islam. They may be Islam-like, parodies of Islam or even mock-heroic misrepresentations of Islam, but they can in no way be Islam proper, that is the spiritual faith which derives its very name from the Arabic word *salām*, meaning peace. The above hypothesis is, as such, not difficult to grasp because as the argument of this volume develops, it constantly carries the above hypothesis within, preserving the fact that such a great global religion is a spiritual faith, neither a political program nor an aggressive form of militancy.

Given the title 'neo-Islam', it may be suggested that such politicized groups are imitations of the original 'heroic' Islam, the Islam of the history school books. It also may imply the 'pseudo-Islam' of the terror groups since they abuse the name of a sublime spiritual faith to mask destructive programs and barbarian behavioral patterns which were already meditated and designed by neo-Islamists for certain purposes. No less significant is the fact that the prefix 'neo', which automatically suggests the modifier 'new', cannot be applicable to religions which are believed to be 'revealed', not man-made, meaning outside the empiricist exertions of the human mind. Revelations are supposed to be heavenly. They are, therefore, absolute. They are not subject to change or to renewal. It is, therefore, inaccurate to speak of a 'new Judaism' or of an 'old Christianity'. Divinity according to the believers in the so-called revealed religions is beyond the reach of human reason, it is absolute, according to religious dogma. To subject the divine to renewal or to modification is practically to tread beyond the sphere of the human space of rationalization, to go 'off limits'. As a term, 'neo-Islam' is ironical.

The purpose behind using this term within the context of this work is, accordingly, self-defining and meaningful because it incorporates, within, its being no Islam. It is consequently meant to be self-defying and, at times, self-refuting.

With reference to the above observations the path to verify the hypothesis that neo-Islam is not Islam becomes obvious. For this purpose one is bound to consult history, to reach back to the original (Islam) for comparisons and contrasts with the partial and, therefore, the inaccurate (neo-Islam).

This volume is divided by the necessity of its argument into two parts: part I. is Islam, the origin which is sought in history for a corrective purpose; and part II., which is neo-Islam, the copy which is the distortive misrepresentation of the faith. The first chapter makes an inquiry into the basic narratives, ideas, misconceptions and misrepresentations which practically contributed to the making of the modern frameworks and formations of neo-Islam. By retreating to the past one may seize the opportunity of discussing the question of whether the founder of Islam, Prophet Muhammed intended the religion which he had conveyed to the people to be a spiritual faith of an individualistic dimension, or a communal bond of people/s unified by a single religious nexus. This complicated question involves discussing the problem concerning how Islam was forced by persecution and suppression in the early years to exchange its essential trait of peaceful proselytizing by the 'word' for the 'sword', bartering persuasion for combat. This leads us to another relevant question concerning whether Islam was meant to be a state or a state-building religion, or simply a spiritual faith.

On his death bed, Prophet Muhammed, the ultimate conveyer and authority of religious knowledge for the early Muslims, neither answered such a question nor did he outline a governance system to cater to the organization of the Muslim community in a state after his death. Hence the schisms that followed. Dissent arose from the absence of a definite, well-meditated and well-organized vision of a communal future existence, a mystery which is not solved definitely to the present day. Such issues are discussed in the first chapter with an eye constantly fixed on how and why Muhammed's companions acted on their own to build a state while he was being buried, implying a redefinition of the faith and making it look something of a national bond and an identity which might be acquired by embracing a religion. The communal nexus superseded the private spiritual dimension, accordingly.

The post-Muhammedan schism produced, among other forms of disagreement, Shi'ism. As it became historically synonymous with opposition, Shi'ism accumulated a mine of anti-establishmentarian practices that consisted of expressions of grievance, disapproval and discontent which, given the state's ruthless suppression, eventually reformulated Shi'ism into a 'religion of protest', though preserving and cherishing its Islamic identity. Shi'i opposition continued unabated to the present day accompanied by the constant violent suppression of the state. Shi'i Islam, therefore, sought undercover political forms of opposition, giving birth to two notable secret organizations that still invite scrutiny for their value as 'models' that were destined to be adapted and adopted in later times by the essentially Sunni neo-Islamic groups. Chapter II is, therefore, devoted to investigate and analyze: (1) The Brethren of Purity, and (2) The Order of the Assassins, with references to their similarities to contemporary neo-Islamic politicized groups that use Islam as mask.

The above historical secret organizations were significant for investigating neo-Islamic terror groups because, though mainly Sunni, they practically provided such groups with Shi'i opposition expertise that had been accumulated through the centuries to be finally used by Sunni neo-Islamic militant groups after the Sunni monopoly of state power was terminated by consecutive waves of triumphant foreign foes.

The second part of the book, 'Neo-Islam', is basically meant to be the antithesis of the first part, 'Islam', making references to the above-noted re-positioning of power-centers which followed the decline of the caliphate. It traces and analyzes the theoretical principles of neo-Islam which were laid down by the Syrian cleric, Ibn Taymiyya (henceforth, Taymiyya) to serve his 'renovation' or the 'renewal' project to rejuvenate the pure, original faith as a corrective social method to restore the Islamic state, with an obliquely implied Sunni Arab leadership.

Conceived from a certain perspective, with today's superheated events and confrontations in mind, neo-Islam, though naively imitative, is misled by its 'prophets' to manufacture a brand new religion, with its practices, programs and future visions which were mostly derived from Taymiyya's intellectual foundations. It is, therefore, no surprise that Wahabi Islam, as an extreme offshoot of the neo-Islamic theory, banishes all the historically established Islamic sects into exile for being not genuinely Islamic. While its puritanical extremism went thus far in alienating and 'infidelizing' other Muslims, Wahabism virtually paved the way for other extremist groups which avowedly adopted terror as the single way to stand up against both the internal and external enemies, namely: the ruling regimes in the Islamic countries and the 'crusading' states of the Western World, to use their favorite terminology. Wahabism first adopted violence on the domestic level by its wars and campaigns inside and outside the Arabian Peninsula, and then by establishing the so-called religious police in contemporary Saudi Arabia, as a terror tool to impose its vision of a deferential society. Empowered by a surplus of state wealth and governmentally licensed clergy, Wahabism then propagated its extremist principles by catering to a mosque-centered educational system which, globalized and generously sponsored, constantly produced young zealots who would qualify to join in the terrorist groups of the *al-Qa'ida* type.

Because neo-Islam began originally as an ancestral dream, the interpretations of the dream proved to be diverse and contradictory at times. In addition to Wahabi extremism, there appeared in Egypt the Muslim Brotherhood which interpreted the Taymiyyan renovation lesson in relatively more moderate terms that had aspired to be both pan-Islamic and relatively progressive in attitude, with a tolerant openness to non-orthodox Muslim groups to substantiate and enhance a global program which was, once again, inspired by the unified neo-Islamic dream of a caliphate, to be the heir and substitute of the late Ottoman one. It distanced itself from the Wahabi hardliners by virtue of its broad worldwide aspirations that required toleration with all Muslims, irrespective of sect, so as to be involved in the contemporary civil political practices, in addition to adhering to its foundation charitable purposes. Yet, the Muslim Brotherhood's long history of anti-government opposition which was continually confronted by suppression, created a fundamentalist trend within the

Brotherhood which might sacrifice politics as civility for violence, a possibility that could be limitlessly destructive, given the huge numbers of its members in and outside Egypt.

On the opposite extreme of the Muslim Brotherhood's version of neo-Islam, the terror groups discarded the moderate path of their fellow Egyptian neo-Islamists in favor of a dogmatic conception of what appeared to such groups to be the enemies of the Islam they profess. Inspired by a dry nomadic conception of social existence and conflict, such extremist neo-Islamists adopted a rather masculine, at times 'sadist', brand of neo-Islam that derived fulfillment and ecstasy from acts of revengeful blind killings, turning their Islam into a Decalogue of repulsive 'do's' and 'don'ts'. With their low opinion of women and womanhood ever present at the back of their minds, such terrorists brag the employment of violence and terror against the above foes, mistaking excessive force for a masculine 'paternal' tool to feminize their enemies, domestic and foreign.

PART ONE

Islam, History

Chapter I

Introductory

After Prophet Muhammed:
The Viability of the State of the Caliphate

One of the most controversial problems that happen to inflict the predominantly Muslim nations of the Middle East stems from the absence of a historically stable and unanimously approved principle on which the institution of an Islamic state may rest to be viable and aspired for in the present and the future. The same observation applies to domestic history which provides no mature model, one which outlines a uniquely Islamic concept of a just state to be recurred to by the Muslim nations as a model and a goal. This is an inherited flaw which has created a perplexing kind of uncertainty in the ideological sense of the expression because this is a constitutional vacuum that has to be filled by a certain theory of state governance, whether borrowed from Western models of capitalism, socialism or from Islamic history which is still a confused and confusing basis of authority and certainty, given the enduring divisions that irritate the world of Islam particularly in the Middle East. Like their ancient, medieval and modern histories which overlap and swerve continually, yielding to no rational or comprehensible pattern of development, the Muslim nations lack consent on a future vision of how their prevalently young states should be run, with an eye on the many divisions (ethnic, sectarian and cultural) which swallow almost all attempts to realize a civil basis of authority. Hence the British and French innovation of the 'mandate' system to justify imposing their rules on the then recently freed nations of the region. The problem of the search for a wise center of authority has a complicated historical dimension that is embedded in the very religion embraced by most of the Middle-Eastern nations.

Because most of those nations were made to mistake history for religion, they discarded their ancient, pre-Islamic, legacies for the European models and clang to religion only for answers, mistaking Islam for the beginning of their histories and presupposing that a spiritual tradition could solve the enigma of the state irrespective of the diverse cultural and religious minority groups, let alone the differences among the Islamic sects themselves. The lately introduced Western models of the state and the government have been conceived by such backward societies as far-fetched theories only. The conceptual flaw crystallized even more painfully when the Arab-centered regimes of the Middle East considered Islam the a 'national' history, irrespective of non-Muslims.

This intellectual dilemma constituted and preserved the ancestral dream which the contemporary Muslim medievalists (henceforth, neo-Muslims) tried to realize, irrespective of the historical, cultural and economical changes that radically remodeled and 're-formed' the world around them, particularly in the last few centuries. It should, therefore, be the incorrect way Islam, which is a spiritual tradition, was received and represented which is to blame for resisting progressive change, turning the question of the state and governance a chronic malady as the ancestral dream became exceedingly obsessive, and inaccessible, especially that it was widely open to interpretations and re-interpretations, formations and re-formations that made the original faith vulnerable to irresponsible modifications and misrepresentations. This tampering with the original spiritual faith, misrepresenting it as a state with an idealized, all-wise government model was one of the flaws to blame for the making and the growth of 'neo-Islam' which deviates far away from the norm of original Islam as it rested in the revelation and in its prophet's traditions because Muhammed never thought of himself as a monarch. In fact, he dismissed being treated like king as irreligious and he never thought of his adherents and companions as constituting a state ruled by an infallible religious law, the *shari'a*. Hence the confusion that followed his death immediately.

I   The Arab in His Environment:

To recreate that case of pre-Islam Arabia within the context of the search for roots, one would be surprised by the emptiness of the Arabian Peninsula which had ever been a wasteland of sand desert. The race that its desert core hosted mirrored the physical emptiness of the environment in its nomadic human and social existence, ever floating aimlessly in a timeless and limitless 'sea' of sand. The ancient Arab nomad (the Bedouin) squeezed the scarce natural resources of the desert hard to obtain the necessary elements for his and his beasts' survival. This is the age-old interdependence between man and beast there. Life was geared with the availability of the rare element of water. Man's existence was thus forever dedicated to the search for, and preservation of water to support his and his domesticated animals' existence. Animals were doubly significant: for transportation and food. The Arab of the desert was essentially egocentric because of this mode of existence: he carried his great grandfather's legacy, "Ishmael was a wild man whose hand was against everyman's".[1] As survival was the ultimate purpose for such a man, significantly called the *Saracen* in ancient and medieval sources, the Bedouin favored a way of life in combination with only small numbers of fellow Bedouins because livelihood used to rely heavily on the individual's physical exertion and endurance, in addition to some seasonal collective work.

Individualism was, therefore, the norm and the essential tenet of nomadic existence out in the open from unmemorable times. It had left its impact deep into the Arab character, crystallizing frequently in the social codes and values of the desert, particularly those of knighthood, hospitality, revenge and the intolerance of the 'eye for an eye'. Arab knighthood was synonymous with the Arab's taste for the poetic and his inclination for the occult, whereas Arab hospitality (for three days only) was the necessity of the vast wilderness where he found himself, and of the sense of aimlessness coupled with the tormenting scarcity of resources. Revenge and vendetta sprang out of the absence of institutions and laws as an individual had to impose his own version of justice in a society with no courts of law and no law enforcement agencies. It ought to be there, in the maze of the hollowness of the limitless deserts that one should dig for the psychological roots of Arab individualism, Arab possessiveness and Arab noncommittal attitude to communal organization, public will and to a commonwealth. Though such qualities might automatically be interpreted as selfish or self-centered, they should concurrently be associated with the Arab's predilection for the imaginative and his pursuance of the occult from times immemorial. Nonetheless, collective social groups or units like the clan and the tribe should have been a later development of early Arab history. Based on the blood nexus, the combination of kinsmen proved to be meritorious for the preservation of life and property. It had begun on a direct familial bond that brought individuals or a small group of blood relatives together to survive and, later, to serve as nucleus for a form of a larger collective existence. The everlasting search for water and pasture proved to be decisive in the formation of authority, no matter how it was, simply because he who had controlled the scarce source of water acquired power and command automatically, exactly like the case of today's peninsula Arabs, except, probably, for the substitution of water by crude oil. Governance and authority were accordingly geared with the control over the sources of wealth, first water and then oil.

That primitive mode of existence which had thus based its conception and awareness of authority was surely free from the sophistications and the age-old traditions and influences of foreign nations which had settled in the fertile lands round Arabia where water was available in abundance as was the case in Mesopotamia, Egypt and the coastal strips of Syria, Arabia Felix, Egypt and Persia.

The age-old and deep-rooted individualism of the original 'wandering Ishmael' persisted in the back of the Arab mind from ancient times as an archetype reminiscent from the existential need and will to survive, a case of survival. By heredity, it was transmitted from generation to generation successively as a dynastic secret code incorporated and diluted into Arab blood. According to Goethe, this primitive mode of human existence squeezed living down to the barest necessities, making the Arab proud of the possession of the tent, the turban and the scimitar,[2] symbolic of his existence in the wilderness. While James Mew adds the 'tale' to Goethe's list of objects to indicate imagination probably,[3] Ralph Waldo Emerson dwells more emphatically on "Religion and poetry",

which are all the civilization of the Arab . . . Religion and poetry, the religion teaches an inexorable destiny: it distinguishes only two days in each man's history, the day of

his lot, and the day of his judgement.[4]

It might be of some significance within this context

to note that in pre-Islam Arabia there were no clear-cut

dividing lines to distinguish the poet, the prophet and, say,

the soothsayer because the three types of persons fell in the

general category of the visionary seer, that is men who had

nothing to do with 'state-building' or with forging a social

contract. This commonplace should apply to Muhammed

who began his religious career as a spiritual teacher with

no ambitions other than teaching the 'Word' of God to the

people, especially in the first phase of his mission. Better

known as the 'Meccan' phase, it was prior to his and his

loyal companions' migration to Medina in 622 A.D. which

was an event of such a formative importance that it was

adopted for the start of the Islamic lunar calendar, the *Hijra*.

Muhammed's original concern was spiritual salvation, the

soul of man, not authority or political power. The Islamic

historical narrative tells us that as part of their attempt to dissuade him and make him forget about his religious message, his opponents, the Meccan fellow citizens, had offered Muhammed their 'presidency' in exchange for giving up. He, however, was said to have declined the generous offer, stating: 'By God, had they put the sun in my right hand, and the moon in my left, to give up this message, I would not have accepted'. This faithfulness and sincerity of purpose to one's belief showed Muhammed, the Christ-like figure who was dedicated to spiritual salvation only.

It was after suffering persecution, ridicule, confiscation of property and attempts of assassination that Muhammed was forced to immigrate from his home town to where the purely spiritual message underwent a radical change in proportionate and violent response to what he and his companions had suffered in the hands of their fellow citizens in Mecca. Islamic proselytizing gave up peaceful persuasion and took to the sword to retaliate. It was at this historical moment in his exile that Muhammed was made a fierce military leader surrounded by an elite of fierce chieftains and martial aides who had been originally vengeful for the loss of their properties and kinsmen back in Mecca. Abruptly, the prophet found himself a community leader, a man in command of a 'community' and a 'church', holding the temporal and the spiritual authorities of his young community. One would wonder how such a great spiritual luminary could be lured into temporal leadership which was supported by martial valor and aggressive stratagem. Note how the erstwhile powerless fugitive turned with his refugee companions into state-builders who were destined to become the inspiration and the future vision for the neo-Islamists who, centuries later, overlooked the peaceful tenets of Islam and stuck to a project of a rejuvenating an Islamic state that was hoped to be founded by their neo-Islam prophets and populated by their fellow neo-Islamists (*al-mujahedūn*) in a dogmatic attempt re-perform the narrative of the medieval theocratic state of Medina that had grown in a totally different era.

Once Muhammed and his followers had built the first mosque in history out of baked clay and date-palm wood, they saw the erected structure as the house of worship and the head quarter of the leadership for lack of resources in the mean time. Hence the vague distinction among the neo-Islamists between matters of the soul and matters of practical life. This vagueness lies at the heart of the dilemma of incomprehension and misunderstanding because for the neo-Islamists spiritual salvation is no matter of good deeds, virtual conduct or prayers, it is rather a matter of channeling the above traits into the effort or the 'struggle' for building an aggressive Islamic state ruled by a 'reproduced' caliphate system. According to their interpretation that ancient mosque was the nucleus of the first Islamic state. In the original narrative, there had been several pressing factors to advocate a masculine aggressive attitude, full of vendetta and revenge sentiments that had pressed hard on the refugees to engender a psychological pressure. It was channeled, not only to establish a utopian Islamic republic of virtuous Muslim men and women, but, more urgently, to militarize that young 'republic' to retaliate against those who had harmed the Muslims before. Thus the sword made its way into Islam as the tool of conversion in place of persuasion since this faith broke away from the limitation of the individual into the broader space of the communal.

With the accumulation of zealous new converts, full of enthusiasm, temperance troops were formed and put under Muhammed's command, forcing the erstwhile powerless fugitive up to the supreme leadership of a community at war. This historical moment further enhanced the conception of Islam not as an individual's faith, but as one of a community, and a rapidly expanding one as well. Islam discarded its former peaceful and individualistic character and became a social bond. This was the consequence of a self-aware and self-contained Muslim community with the domineering presence of a sinless, God-inspired prophet in command. Combination around a heroic figure, enhanced by a kind of arms comradeship, should have generated the aspiration to create a distinct Islamic state consisting of a prophet as an infallible leader and a deferential people unified not by a shared land and, a flag or a constitution, but by a single faith. In a way, this fundamental transformation coincided with the persistent pressure imposed on Muhammed and his companions by an aggressive opposing party which was centered at neighboring Mecca, their birthplace. The consistent fear among the Muslims of being overpowered and attacked by the Meccan 'infidels' added to the solidarity that came out of the sense of a 'new nation' which called itself *ummat al-Islam*, the 'nation of Islam'. It became an identity which had developed unique spiritual and ethical tenets of its own from times of persecution. Vengeance coupled with the availability of enthusiastic swift fighters made it possible now to retaliate against the opposite party by attacking the backbone of its economic superiority, its caravan trade.[5] The consequent comradeship of arms also contributed to the growing sense of combination among the local (Medinan) new converts to Islam, known as the 'supporters' (*al-annsār*) and the erstwhile chased fugitives from Mecca, known as the immigrants (*al-muhajrun*). It eventually showed that the fraternal bond of religion, 'Islamic brotherhood' which had been established by a cause was capable of replacing the old bonds of the tribe, class and trade. As such, it was the sword which the impoverished and weakened Muslims had feared to sway before which created this comradeship and gave it a meaning and a purpose that fed on the certainty of a single fate.

The prophet's presence with his constant and consistent guidelines surely supported the, now, obsessive sense of combination of individuals who had come together from the scattered tribes and the various walks of life. Though he repeatedly stated that "I am but a human being like you", Prophet Muhammed unwittingly stimulated a degree of apotheosis among his companions as a 'sinless' chosen man, simply because admiration might lead to adoration, to recall Thomas Carlyle's theory of the hero.[6] Apotheosis was further assisted by the Muslims' immovable belief that Muhammed was an extension of the revelation and an apparition of divinity since his sayings and behavioral patterns were considered by Muslims inspired and, therefore, part of the revelation.

At the moment Muhammed died after a period of illness, the above apotheosis with all of its implications crystallized by causing unexpected complexities of very many ramifications. The 'power vacuum' he had left with no clearly stated principles or guidelines as to how the 'orphaned' community should rule itself after the departure of its father so as to continue in existence, as a coherent nation (*umma*). The other option was: should the Muslims be dispersed into the wide world as pious individuals with no communal religious role. There was no constitution in the modern sense of the word to assist the durability of a single community unified by a single concept of the state or of the government, one to be entertaining the consent of the majority. This was one of the sources of the superheated conflicting arguments that followed Muhammed's death immediately. As Muhammed, the messenger of God, had left no clear constitutional principles other than general recommendations for the way Muslims should administer their affairs or be ruled as a coherent and uniform social entity, dissent inevitably ensued, stemming from such simple questions as how to define the state and characterize its leader or leadership in such a way as to create a unique system which rejects and deviates from both the ancient domestic tribal traditions of Arabia, and the royal ones of the neighboring kingdoms.

This historical moment of perplexity and uncertainty was surely the most devouring of the many black holes that disrupted Islamic and Middle-Eastern histories, for this matter. The question that followed logically was how could a genius who had founded a distinct community unified by a single faith leave it without a 'prophecy' concerning the issues which were expected to come up after his demise.

Was his nascent Muslim entity a 'kingdom' to be ruled by a monarch to be chosen from the deceased king's kinsmen, or was it a 'republic' to be ruled by an elected president? Islamic histories do make references to the heated controversies and arguments that ensued immediately in the post-Muhammedan period, with reference to the options that were forwarded by the remaining of Muhammed's powerful companions. One option was simply to imitate the neighboring empires. It was dismissed by the majority that clang to the aspiration of creating an unmistakably Islamic state out of the uniqueness of being Islamic as such, being the first of its kind in history.

Because they were still obsessed by the lingering memories of a prophet whom they had considered the seal of prophethood, the above companions innovated the unprecedented system of the 'caliphate' (*al-khelafa*), with the person of the caliph (*khalefa*) on top of it. The stem of the above Arabic word is the verb *khelefeh* (meaning, succeeded or came after). It ultimately indicated that the new leader should be no more than a 'successor' of the prophet to follow in his footsteps. It showed the sense of being still preoccupied by his recent presence. Unfortunately, this personal legacy was destined to yield to the impact of mutation and modification in the course of time. From a certain perspective, being a 'successor' imitating a deceased prophet implied limitations and checks on the new leader's part, making him feel constantly watched, not to say chained. The title of the office aborted the new leader's ease to think freely outside the legacy of a dead man. Although the historically unprecedented title of 'successor' implied such limitations in its early phase, it also implied a degree of sanctity and a sense of superiority that derived from the new leader's exceptionality which arose from his former closeness to the prophet when he had been alive. The dead prophet became the ultimate model and criterion for the living statesmen, realizing a species of eternity by being forever imitated by pious rulers.

To verify the hypothesis that Muhammed had left no clear will or guidelines as to how an Islamic state should be formed after he died, one should shed light on the so-called 'apostasy' that ensued immediately throughout the supposedly 'Islamized' Arabia. The doubts of the Arab tribes were mirrored in the inaugural speech of the first of the prophet's successors, Abu Bakr, as he declared: "If you worship Muhammed; Muhammed is dead; if you worship God; God lives, He never dies".[7] This statement should be read as one which was loaded with reference to groups of Muslims who had deified Muhammed, mistaking him for a Christ-figure. They saw his death as the failure of a vision of eternity.

Another hypothesis deserving of research in this early chapter of Islamic history is the probability that Muhammed breathed his last with the conviction that Islam was a 'spiritual faith', not a state at all. Such a hypothesis might shed some light on the widely held conviction that he had abstained from nominating a successor or an heir to be in charge after his death. This conviction should further support the opinion that he had thought of himself as a God-sent prophet, not the founder of a political entity. His belief in the spiritual message which he had conveyed was made clear in the certainty he expressed while in deathbed to join the biblical prophets who had gone away before him.[8] It might have been one of the most puzzling mysteries of his traditions that, in the last hours of his life, Muhammed was reported to have requested an inkpot and a pen, stating, *'a'atuni dawatan wa qalam'*. His request was denied because, according to some historians, he was known as an illiterate man and such a request was considered by some of his companions a case of 'rambling' in deathbed. Shi'i Muslim historians advocate the hypothesis that he was denied what he had asked for because some of his companions suspected that he might name his cousin, Ali, as the successor. Once again, the 'illiterate prophet' worked wonders even in deathbed.

Irrespective of the mystery that enveloped the above incident, it should still be of significance to allege that no definite governance guidelines had been drawn. That was the reason which made his companions recur to the holy text of the *Qurān* and to the details of his traditions (*al-sunna*) in search of specific clues and clear principles of wise government, misconceiving the prophet as a statesman and the *Qurān* a constitution. The mystery remained at the heart of the grand schism between Shi'is and Sunnis to the present moment: while the former group took the prophet's above-mentioned last request for an attempt to nominate a successor, the latter dismissed the incident as a case of rambling and came out with the innovated 'office' of Muhammed's successor, the caliph. Neither, however, seemed to have contemplated the idea that he probably had no intention of establishing an Islamic state whatsoever. The uncertainty that followed his demise immediately crystallized in the appearance of a number of prophecy claimants who found it opportune to declare themselves as God-inspired prophets of new religious orders like the late Muhammed. They, therefore, refused to pay tax to the newly established state and took to the sword in mutiny. Remembered in Muslim historiography as the 'sham-prophets' and 'sham-prophetesses' (men like Musaylema and women like Sujah), they are now proverbially remembered as synonymous to the word 'lair' in Muslim popular culture. They proved to be staunch opponents to the newly established regime and necessitated violence to deracinate their claims. The so-called *ridda* wars (the wars against the apostates) should serve the inquiring researcher as a touchstone that demonstrated the sham-prophets' dissatisfaction with the regime formulation that grew out of the confusion after the prophet's death. Not only was this chapter of Islamic history kept in the dark by biased historians for political reasons, fresh investigations into it and its background were and are unwelcome by the conservative clerics continually. Also significant is the fact that Shi'i opposition overshadowed such minor and less researched rebellious movements. In later times, Shi'ism obscured other rebels who had ruled supreme in parts of the Arabian Peninsula, rebels who eased Islamic religious duties and declared a revolution against the 'caliph' in Abbasid

Baghdad. The Carmathians (*al-qarāmiṭa*) would pose as an example of the discontent and the civil restlessness with the 'caliphate' as a governance system. Note how Cardinal Newman refers to the Carmathians,

Who pretended to a divine mission to complete the religion of Mahomet, as Mahomet had completed Christianity. They relaxed the duties of ablution, fasting, and pilgrimage; admitted the use of wine, and protested against the worldly pomp of the Caliphs.[9]

The caliphate state regime was in no way uniform or consistent as there appeared three dissimilar major caliphates following Muhammed's death, after the first caliphate had paved the way for the following major ones, two Arab and one Turkish:

The Orthodox caliphate of (*al-rashidun*), who were only four, Abu Bakr, 'Umer, 'Uthman and 'Ali; (2) The Umayyād caliphate (3) ;The 'Abbasid caliphate and (4)

The Ottoman caliphate, the last which ended in 1924. As noted above, the caliphate bodied forth its inconsistency through the above four phases: It began in the first phase as a prevalently 'republican' system in which the caliph was chosen by the majority of the Muslims or their dignitaries. Then it abruptly deteriorated into a monarchy, an Umayyad hereditary monarchy in which the son follows the father to the 'throne'. This hereditary system continued to the end, irrespective of its deviation from the early idealized norm. On the other hand, it began as a strictly Arab and, more specifically 'Qurayshite' (Quraysh), being Muhammed's tribe institution, implicitly forbidden for the non-Arabs (*mawali*), meaning that the caliph had to be an Arab and preferably one of the early companions of the late prophet. The Turkish Ottomans, however, rejected the Arab-centered tradition to justify their hereditary possession of caliphate power, using Muslim jurist justifications made up by clerics close to their court for the purpose, a situation which showed the opportunism of some clerics. Among the other prerequisites for the office of caliph were that the caliph had to be a sane adult (above the age of eighteen), physically fit and free from retarding disabilities such as blindness, in addition to the condition of being a person reputed for religiosity and good manners.

From the above survey, one could conclude with enough confidence that the idea of an Islamic state ruled by an Islamic government had doubtful, shaky and unfixed roots as it had begun in response to a perplexing sense of uncertainty and indecision which engulfed the companions of the late prophet because they clang to a vision of resuming their former experience of a virtuous community under the leadership of a God-sent prophet, a "government of God",[10] to be specific. The vision was bound to fail because the age of infallible prophets was sealed by Muhammed, according to Islamic beliefs; and agreement on a fallible individual was open to varying opinions, assent and dissent. Though it continued for centuries, the caliphate institution underwent changes (as noted above) and it shifted geographically from one center of authority to another (Medina, Kufa, Damascus, Kufa again, Baghdad, Fatimid Cairo, temporarily, and finally Ottoman Istanbul), outlining no fixed or stable center of authority or government that could definitely be characterized as the capital of an 'Islamic' state in the literal meaning of the word. In addition to the Turks' dismissal of the afore-mentioned conditions that had been laid by the early Arab caliphate, the conditions of orthodoxy and orthopraxy began to yield to disregard as early as the Umayyad period in 661 as some of the Umayyād and then Abbasid caliphs were reported to be irreligious, preoccupied with wine, concubinage and courtly pleasures such as soirees, belly dancers and singers who used to be sent from all parts of the vast empire. As for the condition of physical benignity of the caliph, it was abused in the late Abbasid phase by the powerful Buwayhid and, later, Seljuq rulers to dethrone and enthrone the 'puppet' Abbasid caliphs in accordance with their serviceability to the shadow rulers' interests. If one of such rulers wanted to remove a caliph, he would simply blind him by removing one of his eyes' liquids (a process better known in Islamic history as *seml al-'uyoun*) to declare him unfit for the office. This recurrent practice became the horror of the court in the late Abbasid period.

By the time the last of the caliphates (the Ottoman) fell in the aftermath of the First World War, this institution had accumulated a vast legacy of disrepute for totalitarian and irreligious practices to the extent that the new European modes of government, royal and republican, excelled and appeared to be welcome with the European newcomers, the British and French in particular. The Middle-Eastern nations mistook the blond, tall Europeans for missionaries of progress, democracy and liberty.

The caliphate, as an institution, is idealized now by the active political neo-Islamic groups which, following in the footsteps of earlier neo-Islamic theorists like Taymiyya, clang only to the first phase of the historical caliphate, that of the above-mentioned 'republican' four orthodox caliphs whose reigns were by no means free from troubles and political conflict.

It should be noteworthy that, irrespective of its historically proven inconsistencies and pitfalls, the caliphate is idealized by most of the neo-Islamist political groups, except probably for the Shi'i ones, not only because, so they think, it was the closest to the primitive Islam that had been modeled after the persona of Prophet Muhammed and his companions, but also because it witnessed the golden age of 'missionary Islam' outside Arabia, the age of the conquests.

Chapter II

Secret Societies in Islamic Political History

The assassination of Caliph Ali (661 A.D.) marked the end of his and his followers' (the Shi'is) brief term in power for about five years only that were whipped by turmoil and instability. It also marked the eclipse of Shi'ism into the hazy world of political opposition and secrecy, the one that showed up every now and then in later periods in the forms of intermittent violent outbreaks and uprisings, beginning with that of Ali's own son, al-Husayn, which the new Umayyād hereditary caliphate (661-750 A.D.) crushed ruthlessly in 680 A.D. Thenceforth Islamic history turned into a saga of rebellions, revolutions and suppressions which, coupled by the worldwide conquests, kept on reminding the center of authority as well as the careful historiographer that there, indeed, was something wrong with the political system which continued long enough to the end of the Arab caliphate of the Abbasids (750-1258 A.D.) who followed in the footsteps of their Umayyād predecessors.[1] Nowhere was this longish and violent chapter of Islamic history more eloquently mirrored than in an old man's speech to an Umayyād caliph after crushing one of the outbreaks. It captivates Washington Irving's pioneer, though forgotten history of Islam as he quotes that old man, stating

"I am fourscore and ten years", said he, "and have outlived many generations, In this very castle I have seen the head of Hosein presented to Obeid'allah, the son of Ziyad; then the head of Obeid'allah to Al Mokhtar; then the head of Al Mokhtar to Musab, and now that of Musab to yourself. The Caliph was superstitious, and the words of the old man sounded ominously as the presage of a brief career to himself. He determined that his own head should not meet with the similar fate within the castle's walls, and gave orders to raze the noble Citadel of Cufa to the foundation.[2]

The recurrent bloody rebellions were no more than the visible tip of the iceberg of social protest and public grievances which hid deep beneath to embark on secret activities, groups and militias that mirrored the grievances and goals of the Shi'is.

The failure of both of the Arab caliphates (Umayyād and Abbasid) was embodied by their inability to achieve some kind of political unanimity capable of preventing further dissent and political unrest like those of the Kharejites (those who had dissented from Ali's camp of Shi'is), and the Carmathians (*al-qaramiṭa*) who captivated Cardinal Newman's attention for their significant representation of the intellectual discontent concerning the center of authority and for their embodiment of protest, not only against the state, but also against the whole paradigm of the religious authority it had claimed to stand for:

What is relevant to my purpose in the Saracens is, that their quarrels often had an intellectual basis, and arose out of

35

their religion. The white, the green, and the black factions, who severally reigned at Cardova, Cairo, and Baghdad, excommunicated each other, and claimed severally to be the successors of Mahomet. Then came the fanatical innovation of the Carmathians, who pretended to a divine mission to complete the religion of Mahomet, as Mahomet had completed Christianity. They relaxed the duties of ablution, fasting, and pilgrimage; admitted the use of wine, and protested against the worldly pomp of the Caliphs. They spread their tents along the coast of the Persian Gulf, and in no long time were able to bring an army of 100,000 men into the field. Ultimately they took up their residence on the borders of Assyria, Syria, and Egypt. As time went on, and the power of the Caliphs still further reduced, religious contention broke out in Bagdad itself, between the rigid and the lax parties.[3]

Shi'i opposition was by no means uniform as it had undergone splits and produced ramifications either for internal political disagreements or for doctrinal differences.

On such differences were blamed the appearance, within the Shi'i opposition, of the Isma'ili Shi'is (also known as the fivers for their belief in five imāms, instead of twelve, like the twelvers). Those Isma'ili Shi'is constituted a particularly notable opposition group for their secretive ways and for their highly complicated organization, let alone their contributions to the making of a mysterious fraternity, the Brethren of Purity, and for their making and organization of one of the most notorious terrorist groups in the history of Islam, the Order of the Assassins. In the first instance, the fraternity had shown surprising similarities to freemasonry, while in the second; the Assassins virtually foreran the contemporary terror organizations in a number of ways that deserve consideration.

*The Brethren of Purity; or the Basra Masons:

Although there were several secret opposition groups unified by their anti-establishmentarian orientation, none was so sophisticated, secretive and highly organized like the Brethren of Purity, *ikhwan al-safa*, (henceforth, the Brotherhood, or the Brothers for its members). In its recruitment of members of all shades of belief all and social ranks, it transcends the alleged Shi'i sma'ili coloration which had, probably stuck to it during its founding period (during the reign of the Shi'i dynasty of the Buwaihids of the late Abbasid period) to continue being synonymous with it ever since. The Brotherhood seemed to have stripped this alleged limited sectarian identity in time through its recruitment of a broad spectrum of members from almost all walks of life and all specializations to the extent that one is tempted to stress its parallelisms to Freemasonry. The Brotherhood echoed sonorously the secrecy of the Freemason 'clan' in its strong emphasis on the tight confidentiality concerning its rituals, organization and, over all, the secret identities of its member. No less significant was the emphasis it laid on the fraternal bond that combined all of its members together, irrespective of their ranks within its internal hierarchy.[4] The Brotherhood's hierarchy, though graded age wise, paused another parallelism to Masonry as its staircase begins with the rank of the 'craftsman', or the 'Loyal and the Compassionate' (Arabic, *abrar/ruhama'*), the lowest rank, and it ascends upward to the 'Royal' rank, the highest of the ranks which was also known as the rank of the 'Prophets and Philosophers'. While the craftsman could be any mature individual (fifteen years old or more) who was known for his honesty and compassion, the highest of the ranks (fifty years or more) indicated luminaries like the prophets and the philosophers of the standing of Prophet Muhammed, Socrates', or geniuses of similar value to humanity, which was an obvious indication of one of the Brotherhood's purposes of purifying tainted and distorted religion by philosophy.[5] In between, there was the rank of the 'Good and Noble' (Arabic, *akheyar/ fudhala'*),who were well versed in policies (thirty years and more) and the rank of the 'Noble and Generous'(Arabic, *fudhala'/ kiram*) the one for of the kings and sultans (forty years and more).

Such nominations were, of course, emblematic, not literal.

The only document that was left by the Brotherhood to posterity is a great anonymous written work which consists of a number of philosophical treatises and intellectual discourses, each put under the title of 'epistle', compromising the whole book, *The Epistles of the Brethren of Purity* (henceforth, *The Epistles* (Arabic: *rasā'il ikhwan al-safa)*. Note how it is justifiable, not to say feasible, to compare the Brotherhood to Freemasonry through observing *The Epistles'* anonymous author/compiler's authoritarian survey of the Brotherhood's membership which is quoted at length below at length for its indicative, documentary value, addressing the reader directly:

know that among us there are kings, princes, khalifs, sultans, chiefs, ministers, administrators, tax agents, treasurers, officers, chamberlains, nobles, servants of kings and their military supporters. Among us too there are merchants, artisans, agriculturists and stock breeders. There are builders, landowners, the worthy and wealthy, gentlefolk and possessors of all many virtues. We also have persons of culture, of science, of piety and of virtue. We have orators, poets, eloquent scholars, jurists, judges, magistrates and ecstatics. Among us too there are philosophers, sages, geometers, astronomers, naturalists, physicians, diviners, soothsayers, casters of spells and enchantments, interpreters of dreams, alchemists, astrologers, and many other sorts, too many to mention.[6]

If the above excerpt is not enough to verify the hypothesis concerning the Brotherhood's affinity with Freemasonry, the anonymity of its members is, because it further reiterates the same conclusion. The Brotherhood's lengthy title may be of no less significance for its cloudy and vague nature: 'The Brethren of Purity and Companions of Loyalty, the Praised People and Glory's Children'(Arabic: *ikhwan al-safa wa khullan al-wafa wa ahl al-hamd wa abna' al-majd*).

The Brotherhood was a tenth-century phenomenon that flourished in Basra, south of the point where the Tigris and the Euphrates merge to form the Shatt al-Arab waterway that flows into the Arabian/Persian Gulf. It seems to be the ultimate outcome of the confluence of various, seemingly contradictory philosophical and spiritual trends which happened to meet and interact previously, during the so-called golden age of the Arab-Islamic civilization which had matured a few centuries before. The tenth century was also a period that saw the decline of the Abbasid Baghdad caliphate that coincided with the rise of two peripheral Shi'i entities, the Zaydi in Yemen (901 and after) and the Fatimid in Tunisia, and then in Cairo. In response to an era of turmoil and political instability, the Brotherhood might have paused as the only stable entity which was destined to organize a unique combination of the intellectual and social elites to shield its members from the blind and violent storms of an age of turmoil, the storms that had led to the execution of the great mystic, the Sufi Mansour al-Hallaj, for the heresy of stating: "I am the Truth".[7] Such mystic ideas, together with the impact of Aristotelian logic and Neo-Platonist orientations of the Brotherhood were destined to be fruitful in a conservative social milieu that was ridden by the traditional custodians of religion. In such times of paradox and uncertainty, secrecy was an act of safety and self-protection, particularly for the Shi'i opposition which had adopted dissimulation (*taqia*) to avert persecution and escape such fatal accusations as those which had victimized the afore-mentioned Sufi, Mansour al-Hallaj, publically.

The suspicions that hovered round the Brotherhood for its alleged Shi'i roots, in addition to the ideas it propagated, could well justify the problem of the authorship and authenticity of its best known work, *The Epistles*, because of the common allegation that it had been the product of the 'Hidden Imām', a Shi'i messianic figure, supposedly in occultation then and now. He was, as ever, expected by the Shi'is to stage a comeback to redeem the world. No less significant in this respect are the 'hidden' names of the 'compilers' or authors of *The Epistles* who were said to have gone into a secret 'cave' for a hideout to escape the eyes of the authorities and avoid the antipathy of the traditional pro-caliphate clerics. They were reported to have done so, not to protect themselves, to protect their God-given talents. They were mythologized as they were supposed to have stayed in that metaphorical 'cave' till the time was appropriate for them to uncover their identities and real beliefs.[9] In this case, the suggestion of a hidden imām who had gone into a timeless cave, symbolic of the occultation seemed tenable. Although meant to perplex and camouflage, such legends concerning the identity of *The Epistles'* author or compiler was surely inspired by the mine of Shi'i, especially Nizari Isma'ili, apocalyptic beliefs, a hypothesis that has been embraced by a number of significant contemporary scholars devoted to the field such as A.A.A. Fayzee, Richard Netton, Yeves Marquet and Bernard Lewis.[10] A contemporaneous local scholar, known by the name of Ibn Qifti (d. 1248) further deepened the uncertainty as he, once again, ascribed *The Epistles* to one of the infallible imāms of Ali's line. As such, the anonymity of *The Epistles'* author or compiler was actually an extension of the anonymity of the Brotherhood's members who are not yet identified accurately even by contemporary scholarship except for a few names.

If examined impartially and with a bias-free approach, the Brotherhood would crystallize before the beholder to be too universal and inclusive to be inserted into the narrow slot of a certain religion, sect or creed. Note the Brotherhood's all inclusive universality in the characteristic traits of the ideal person as illustrated in *The Epistles,* according to the best prevalent criteria of that era. The ideal person should accordingly be

of East Persian derivation, of Arabic faith, of Iraqi, that is Babylonian education, Hebrew in astuteness, a disciple of Christ in conduct, as pious as a Syrian monk, a Greek in natural sciences, an Indian in the interpretation of mysteries

and above all a Sufi or a mystic in his whole spiritual outlook.[11]

Equipped with the best of every faith and culture from ancient Greece to ancient India, the outcome was bound to be a millennial 'superman', the offshoot of a unified humanity. Put into the wide matrix of a membership which combined people of all professions, trades and crafts, the Brotherhood broke away from all limited exclusive categories of religion, ethnicity or class. Literally inclusive of 'every man', it magnified its invisible power which might have ruled supreme in an era of civil unrest and a weak center of authority. The Brotherhood's power might have been compensatory and regulatory, embedded in its concealed leadership which seemed to be capable of imposing whatever was fitting to its vision, particularly that the secret organization included monarchs and powerful government dignitaries who belonged to foreign states from outside the Islamic caliphate. As such, it constituted a species of an 'international government'.

One is bound to believe that the Brotherhood's brand of transcendentalism and avowed 'cosmic consciousness', that which made its members keen on reciting a 'cosmic text' at night and in the open with their faces directed to the polar star, would appear incomprehensible and probably heretic in the eyes of the simple people who populated Basra and the other cities during that unstable era at the verge of a longish period of decadence. Hence the accusations of heresy, infidelity set against the Brotherhood and its members. Such accusations were enough excuse for *The Epistles'* author/compiler to seek refuge in the concealment of the above-mentioned 'metaphorical' cave, a hideout which had originally been inspired by *Qur'ānic* and Biblical narratives.

As a globalized and globalizing organization, the Brotherhood could well be conceived as the covert equivalent or offshoot of another official institution that had been formerly founded by the Abbasid caliph al-Ma'mun for the Arabicization of the other nations' gems of culture and science, that institution which was significantly called 'The House of Wisdom', *bayt al-hikma*. The Baghdad caliph's establishment and patronage of this institution in addition to his keenness on bringing the best minds of the age to its service paused as an early proof that he had been fully aware of the fact that 'knowledge is power,' because he desired to lock the supremacy of world civilization within cosmopolitan Baghdad through the combination and inclusion of the intellectual products of the best minds from the seemingly opposing philosophies and worldviews of the various cultures, past and contemporaneous. But for the translators of the House of Wisdom, the masterpieces of Greek and Roman philosophy, Indian legacy and Far-Eastern letters might have been lost to later generations, particularly in Europe. In a way, by introducing such ideas and intellectual treasures into Arab-Islamic culture, the House of Wisdom set the contemporaneous mind free from the fetters of a domineering and authoritative religion. As a landmark in world cultural history, it had a far stronger impact on domestic culture. Put in this perspective, the Brotherhood might be conceived as the outcome of the earlier Abbasid cultural openness which had been forced by the above-mentioned caliph who, though remembered for Shi'i leanings, was captivated by the vision of preserving and maintaining world supremacy., Though 'secret', the Brotherhood echoed a former period of wholesale intellectual and cultural interaction of a relatively lasting impact. Its *Epistles* mirrored the above conclusion for it tackled conventionally tabooed ideas and brought to discussion subjects such as those of disambiguation (Arabic, *qadariyya*), esotericism, neo-Platonism, in addition to discussing forbidden questions concerning the role of the revelation and human existence.[12]

The very mention of such terms and topics as the above was tabooed and misconceived as blasphemous and, therefore, anti-establishmentarian. They were enough to accuse those who risk discussing them of apostasy, infidelity or heresy by the conservative custodians of the religious tradition whose interests might be threatened by such 'outrageous topics'. This was the cause behind the strict confidentiality of the Brotherhood, to be sure. It was for such insecure circumstances that the Brotherhood had to go secret in a rebellious gesture to break away from the fossilized shell that had encapsulated culture and pressed hard on the free minds of the intellectual elite. The Brotherhood might have acquired its Isma'ili coloration from the religious persuasion of some of its outstanding members and founders, but this limitation should never be seen as an immovable ceiling which it could not transcend to soar high in the wider orbits of the trans-ethnic and trans-religious space. There was something indisputably Masonic in its secrecy, traditions, ritual, membership gradation and, overall, in the fraternal nexus it established among its members. Its sectarian identity could have been used as a curtain to hide its real identity as an anti-institutional reinvigoration of an ancient secret society in tenth-century Basra, hypothetically the birthplace and home of the fictitious character of Sinbad the Sailor. It might be notable in this respect that the first Masonic lodge in modern Iraq was also founded in Basra.

*The Assassins

Perhaps the Order of the Assassins pauses as the closest historical precedent to the contemporary neo-Islamic terror groups. The Order's secrecy, deliberate spread of terror, religious identity and sectarian extremism, among other qualities, all indicate the parallelisms which can be found in radical neo-Islamic terror organizations today. The term 'assassins' is full of meaning: it is originally Arabic (a derivation from the stem *hashish*, meaning angelica or weed); and an assassin is originally a *hashāsh*, a *hashish* taker or addict.[13] They were the enemies of the members of the order who chose the above name 'Assassins' for them to distort their reputation as hashish addicts, who were usually looked down at as individuals out of wits, were seen to be controlled not by sensible reason but by substance abuse. The Assassins were known within the Order's internal circle as the *faddawiya* or *feda'iyeen*, meaning persons who were ready to sacrifice their lives for the Order's cause. In other words, the Assassins were, probably, the earliest predecessors of the suicidal killers in the history of Islam. It was the common opinion during the prime of their terrorist activities that the Assassins were chosen young men who were provided with *hasheesh* by the Order's most charismatic and most memorable leader, Hasan al-Sabbah (1037-1124) who meant to achieve full control of his disciples.

A new recruit was convinced, one way or another, that his life was meant to be spiritually sacrificial. Thus he had to be shown one or more of the *faddawiywa* ordered by Hasan al-Sabbah to jump from a high, sharp cliff into an unfathomable valley as a demonstration of their fidelity and their readiness for the ultimate sacrifice. The Assassins were also said to have been provided with *hashish* to have a prior taste of the Qur'anic *Jenna* (paradise) promised by God for the faithful as a reward so that they would welcome death as a swift shift to that everlasting paradise. Sabbah's total control of his Assassins stemmed from this promise as it triggered other narratives and spawned various tales such as his purposeful making of a replica of the promised paradise on earth in one of the neighboring green valleys, an orchard that was allegedly provided with streams of honey and others of wine, complete with the prettiest young women *hour al-'eyn* (the pretty-eyed), inspired by the Qur'ā'nic paradise (*jenna*) imagery, to cater to the believers' needs and wild desires. To be sure, this make-belief paradise was manufactured centuries before Hollywood. Some aggressive historiographers went so far as to consider Hasan al-Sabbah the devil in disguise for his irresistible persuasive abilities and the consequent full mastery of his disciples.

During his leadership of the order and after, the Assassins became the terror of the ruling and powerful elites of the Islamic world, particularly because they missed no one of their 'targets', whether a Muslim ruler, a cleric or a crusader. Once a man of power made an unfriendly gesture or an aggressive declaration against the 'Nizari' Islma'ili sect of the Assassins, he should automatically expect that he would be black-listed in the Order's targets as an enemy of the sect. The intolerable terror such a target suffered, once aware or made aware of his offence, originated from the offender's certainty that he would be assassinated in the most tormenting way, in public and by a dagger.[14] No less horrifying were the treacherous and maneuvering methods the Assassins habitually adopted to reach the 'target' in his court or in a seemingly safe place, no matter how long would the penetration process take. They first used to make sure that they had won the full trust of their future victim, and then they would specify the best moment to stab him in a public place to awe the by-standers and send the horrifying message to the widest public. Jefferson Gray relates one such terrifying murder which was executed by two Assassins who had penetrated into the court of Conrad of Montferrat, a crusade leader, in the guise of Arab Christian monks.[15] Ever aware of their bloody fate in the hands of the Assassins, dignitaries who had done the Assassins or their sect harm would have to live the terror of abrupt stabbing for the rest of their lives till they fatally meet the dagger with their chests one day. The dagger became a specter that hovered in the air round the already weakened victim till he was relieved for good by the tangible one. The very sight of a dagger put close to a person's dwelling conveyed a warning message to the following victim, implying that 'You are next'.[16]

Although Bernard Lewis surveys several dissimilarities between the Assassins and their present-day terrorist successors, including the current indiscriminate killings (allegedly for religious reasons), the tools of murder and the Assassins' prior warning to their victims, among others[17], it should be of significance to point out as well the overwhelming similarities between the two groups of terror, the old and the new. Both base and justify their terrorist 'operations' by religious causes, both are suicidal, both capitalize on hypnotized assassins who are driven by the hallucination of a reward after death and both rely on promoting an atmosphere of fear. In the historical case, the Assassin expected to go to the Qur'anic paradise he had formerly tasted on earth in his life time, while in the contemporary case the suicidal bomber is said to be sure that he would 'dine' with Prophet Muhammed once he dies willingly for the cause.

Any survey of the political history of Islam is bound to identify political opposition, its ramifications, rhetoric and outbreaks with Shi'ism because it had originally grown out of an undecided and unresolved question of state power, its form and devolution, a situation which is still unresolved between the nostalgic Shi'is and Sunnis. Ever persecuted and ruthlessly suppressed by the traditionally Sunni states of the caliphate, the opposition pursued various ways to accomplish its goals and pursue its programs with a specific emphasis on to the making of secret groups and organizations which would either impact the status quo indirectly by intellectual and civil means, or directly by adopting terror and violence to fulfill their purposes. The significance of the historical lesson crystallizes today in the survival or revival of modes of opposition, the peaceful and the lethally violent.

PART TWO

Neo-Islam

Chapter III

The Making and Growth of Neo-Islam: From Taymiyya to Wahabism

I. A Historical Preview: Islam, From Persuasion to Compulsion:

As noted in the first chapter, most of the histories of Islam demonstrate the fact that, as a communal religious tradition, Islam did yield to change through time and in harmony with the succession of the ages and their novelties, let alone the modifications introduced by tyrants and their clerical organs, the turbaned custodians of religion in accordance with the interests and perspectives of the various religious groups in varying social milieus, particularly after Islam's extension into all directions, far enough to become one of "the great religions of the world".[1]

One may note the labels assigned by historians and religion scholars to the successive phases Islam went through, from its advent (roughly before 622 A. D.) down to the present day, to mark the above-mentioned changes which came out in accentuation with the successive novelties. That is why some such scholars justifiably write on 'primitive Islam', 'medieval Islam' and 'modern Islam', let alone 'black Islam' or 'American Islam'. The early phase which is identified with the presence of Prophet Muhammed (570-632), his early companions and, then with reigns of the four orthodox successors (the *caliphs*) is usually named by Muslim historians as 'the early phase of Islam' (Arabic, *sadr al-Islam*). It includes the narrative of the abrupt breaking of the revelation by the Angel Gabriel (*jubra'il*) to Muhammed and the prophet's declaration of a religious 'message', accordingly. The phase also includes the thrilling stories of the first responders out of whom the above-mentioned successors were chosen to rule the young Islamic community (*umma*) after Muhammed's death consecutively. As demonstrated in the first chapter, this formative phase is traditionally subdivided into two periods. The earlier period saw the early Muslims as a powerless group of persecuted individuals who suffered the maltreatment and persecution of the idolatrous majority. The Muslims were few fugitives who relied for their guidance and secret proselytizing on a spiritual belief propagated by an illiterate, though charismatic, prophet who had declared himself an inspired 'messenger' from God. This initial period marked commitment to the original tenet of Islam, the religion of peace. The latter Medinan period marked the fundamental development of Islam into a militant faith, once it adopted the dictum of the 'eye for an eye' towards those who had victimized the early peaceful converts. At Medina, their asylum, the early Muslims discarded persuasion for the propagation of their new religion in favor of the sword, encountering the idolatrous pagans with the condition of: 'either embrace Islam, or die fighting'. Literally stated, 'Embrace Islam, and save yourself'. This command did not, however, apply to the Jews and Christians (*ahl-al-kitab*) as believers in revealed monotheistic religions, unless they wished to convert to Islam voluntarily, of course.

The above two periods are glorified by almost all Muslim historians, not only for the prophet's domineering presence (as a second source of the revelation, with the *Qur'ān*), but also for being the period when the pure original religion was still untainted by alien beliefs and practices. Subdivided into peaceful and militant periods, this early phase is, therefore, referred to by some historians as the phase of 'early Islam', meaning Islam *par excellence*, for this matter.

Sunni Muslim historians tend to emphasize the extension of the above idealized prophetic period to merge into the period which followed Muhammed's death, assuming that the reigns of the so-called four orthodox caliphs (*al-rashidūn*) (632-661 A.D.) were no less pure and religiously committed to the original tenets of the faith. It witnessed the rapid growth of Islam into a state, complete with an essentially unique citizenry which had made a nation of itself, one which was unified by a single faith (though it contained some non-Muslims, *ahl al-thima*). The young state was given the name of 'the caliphate', mirroring the alleged fact that it was ruled by a supreme leader whose authority was originally derived from his status of being a successor of Muhammed, the Prophet of God.

Though the above idealized two periods (with and without Muhammed's presence) were by no means fault-free, they still were held with great reverence by both Shi'is and Sunnis, in spite of the former group's objections and its consequent dissent.[2] This 'great schism' in Islam marked the growing incongruity between the two groups, demonstrating the 'mutiny within' clearly.

It was the following Umayyad dynasty's caliphate

(662-750) that failed the promising prospects of the above early phase due to turning the caliphate royal instead of the former republican system when the caliph had to obtain the assent of the majority of believers to assume power. The change the Umayyads inaugurated was disapproved by most of the Muslims and most of their historians as it marked the beginning of the deterioration which engulfed the ruling institution as a government system, particularly that the hereditary transition of the caliphate was later reiterated by being followed by the Abbasids (750-1258), the Fatimids (909-1171) and the Ottomans (1299-1923). It was only World War I that terminated the caliphate for good as an allegedly 'Islamic' state.

II. The Justifications of Neo-Islam:

Originally, neo-Islam began as a religious intellectual stance that, embittered by the deterioration of the Islamic state, aspired to revive it by imitating only the earlier idealized phase of the four orthodox caliphs in Islamic history, excluding the subsequent phases, no matter how accomplished and urbane they had been. Lured into this revivalist vision, all neo-Islamists yearned to re-establish the 'caliphate' as an Islamic state in charge of all Muslims even if they were outside its borders. The essential vision was, therefore, imitative in nature as it appealed to a by-gone historical phase which survived only in the dust-gathering chronicles and in the revivalists' minds, those minds which overlooked all the changes and developments that kept on taking place continually ever since the end of that idealized phase. This might be the reason why they looked like dreamers for some Muslims because they asked for too much within an opposing, forward-looking environment, especially that the dream was essentially regressive.

Also notable in this context is the fact that neo-Islam is the offshoot of the ages of turmoil and cultural decadence for it began and continued to be synonymous with orthodox

Sunni Islam after it had lost power in front of the thrust of ferocious foreign foes. Unfortunately, neo-Islam's program seems to fail in its most important pan-Islamic vision by excluding a huge portion of the world's Muslim population, the Shi'a. They, therefore, maintain a totally different vision, an apocalyptic compensatory Messianic one.[3] As such, neo-Islam sorts the Shi'a out, alienates and antagonizes them, carrying in its sweeping torrent the antithesis of its ultimate vision of a united Muslim *umma*. Ironically, the neo-Islamists get carried away by the nostalgic vision, anticipating a day when all Shi'is would undergo a heart change and embrace the basically Sunni neo-Islamic vision in a wholesale manner. Alienating the Shi'a resulted in creating an internal enemy, echoing the original problematic of the historical narrative that had witnessed Shi'i dissent right after Muhammed's departure.

III. Taymiyya: Laying the Foundations of Neo-Islam:

The above flaw in neo-Islamic programs and attitudes dates back to the works of the originator of the neo-Islamic theory, a Syrian cleric known by the title of *Shaykh al-Islam*, who was better known by the name of Ibn Taymiyya (1263-1328). From the records that are available today concerning Taymiyya's life and works, one may conclude that he was a clever, encyclopedic man in line with all the learned men of his time, particularly that he is said to have mastered arithmetic, algebra, philosophy, logic and jurisprudence, of course. He distinguished himself by developing a system of persuasive polemics addressed to the Islamic peoples to rescue them from decadence. He was originally urged by the widespread deterioration and decay that had engulfed the erstwhile glorious Islamic state and peoples and made them easy preys to foreign intrusion. He, therefore, concluded that only a return to the undisturbed sources of Islam, the model of the early 'good ancestors' (*al-salaf al saleh*) could restore Islam and Muslims to their purity and, therefore, to the early ideal Islamic state, the caliphate. As such, he established one of the distinctive features shared by of all Sunni neo-Islamic groups, their belief in reinstituting the caliphate, or the Islamic state. Hence the current idiomatic use by the salafists (*al-salafia*) of the slogan 'The caliphate is the answer', to indicate that very retrospective and regressive attitude and those who embrace it for their obsession with a medievalist ancestral dream. He enthroned Prophet Muhammed, his companions and their followers or disciples to the third generation as the purest models who had literally to be 'copied' for a rejuvenation of essential Islam, community and state (*umma* and caliphate). Though tempting and inspiring to all truant Muslims, Taymiyya's revivalist endeavor rejected all that had been contemplated and said by Muslims and their clerics before. Instead, he adopted only two sources of immovable and absolute authority, the text of the holy *Qurān* and the traditions of Muhammed (*al-Sunna*).[4] Those should be the yardstick against which all issues and former edicts or opinions should be measured and valued continually for the accuracy of the religious law (*al-shari'a*) and the proper administration of the Muslim faith.

By this argument, Taymiyya automatically passed an intolerant verdict against all practices, convictions edicts and religious opinions that had appeared in the course of time, considering them suspect for being baseless innovations and accretions (*bida'*), especially when they did not conform by the above two authorities in a literal sense. The predilection to strict sternness was originally justified and instigated by the Mongol pagan invasion of Muslim regions, on the basis that tolerating the causes of decay, the man-made innovations and additions to the original religion in particular, would inevitably repeat the vicious circle that had weakened Islam, terminated the Baghdad caliphate (1258) and engulfed the Muslims, making them vulnerable to invasions by primitive nomadic tribes like those of the Tartars. If this was the timely incentive behind Taymiyya's neo-Islamic theory, it should have been the impassable bar between heaven and earth, the revelation and reason that dictated to him the limits of human reason in its endeavor to exceed the divine that had been revealed in the holy book and the prophet's traditions. Taymiyya's idealization of the first three Muslim generations that followed Muhammed stemmed from their very commitment to the revelation and to the prophet's traditions and, of course, to this commitment's eventual rejection of the exertion of the human mind (*ijtihd*) which tampered with what was beyond its limits, the divine. The human mind should deal only with ordinary and earthly facts, not with the absolute Truth which is the territory of a greater Intelligence. His polemic was taken up, extended and elaborated by later Islamic renovators who reiterated his theses on the purity of the early ancestors to support the same endeavor for commitment to the Truth that is embedded in the revelation, discarding transitory empiricism.

As he thought that he had grasped the *elixir Vita* for

Islam's everlasting youth in the above formula, Taymiyya

and his imitators proceeded on an authoritative process of

value judgments, surveying almost every common belief

or supposedly established practice, including assessing

Muslim groups and sects that cherish such 'innovated'

beliefs and 'alien' practices or rituals. They, however, came

out with a list of 'black-and-white' evaluations. Thus it

became practically tenable for them to dismiss whatever

seemed to them not conforming by the ultimate criteria he

had set up, the holy book and the traditions of the prophet.

Taymiyya and his disciples classified the religiously harmful

and hateful in two hazy categories: (1) The assignment of

a partner to God or to His divine tenets (Arabic, *al-shirk*),

and (2) The innovation of a notion or a practice which had

not been followed by the above-indicated early Muslims

(Arabic, *al-bide'*). Also notable among his consequential

conclusions was the one which stated that Islam is the

ultimate religion, as Muhammed is the seal of prophethood,

dismissing the Jews and Christians outside the territory of

salvation, and disregarding the age-old tolerance allotted to them which had been established by the prophet himself. More relevant to his impact on contemporary terror was his conclusion that whatever came from both religions, whether states, persons or organizations, should be suspected of being harmful to Muslims.[5] Thus, he had paved the way to the subsequent blind anti-Western rejection of Western 'products' or practices characteristic of later neo-Islamist groups. In line with Taymiyya's guidelines, they conceived such products as parts of the latter day's 'crusade' aiming at the termination of Islam and its believers altogether.

He was no less intolerant with fellow Muslims, including the Shi'a and the *sufi* mystics among other groups for their nonconformist practices and beliefs. Taymiyya beheld the Shi'a as extremist enthusiasts for their sanctification of their imāms, while he condemned the *sufis* for reviving Gnostic ecstasies and imitating monastic practices that distance them from the path to God.

Taymiyya's emphasis on Islam's uniqueness and, of

course, 'superiority' to other revealed religions could have been a conclusion obtained from the dissimilarities of such religious systems to Islam, a situation that might have paved the way for the neo-Islamic inherent antagonism to the West, particularly after the latter's aspirations in the Islamic regions unraveled through the crusades, a historical collision that made the Muslim mind identify the Western World with Christianity. Taken to extremes, Taymiyya's anti-Christian and anti-Jewish argument provided a backdrop for subsequent neo-Islamic cautious interactions and encounters with Western states and cultures because the neo-Islamists whom Taymiyya had forerun shrank into an unbreakable xenophobic shell to protect the self from the sweeping tides of Western thought and its new ideas. To hammer this shell would, therefore, be interpreted as a harmful, not to say treacherous action to the original faith and to the interests of its adherents, accordingly.

Taymiyya's idealization of the early Islamic phase automatically implied a parallel idealization of the mode of government that the 'virtuous ancestors' had established. The early caliphate was, accordingly, made an ultimate goal to aspire for by the neo-Islamists. Foreign models of civil or secular government were, of course, to be suspected and discarded even when they catered to such captivating slogans as democracy, liberty and human rights. As the aspiration to revive the caliphate became a unifying belief for all neo-Islamists from Taymiyya on to today's terror groups, this whole aspiration turned xenophobic because it blindly suspected all that came from Europe or the foreign world in general. Although they did embrace Islam after storming the heartland of the Asian core of the Islamic world, the Mongols remained a suspect source of legislations in the eyes of Taymiyya due to their ancient pagan traditions.[6] This stance verifies Taymiyya's rejection of everything foreign, irrespective of the source, whether it was good or harmful. His low opinion of the Mongols, though no more pagan, carried an element of a xenophobic, Arab-centered chauvinism which was destined to be consequential, particularly in the contemporary Arab low opinion of non-Arab Muslims (*mawali*).[7] This bias would later be utilized by pan-Arab nationalist movements as an 'Islamic' argument against the European aspirations in the Middle East, not to mention its utility for the myth of 'Arab superiority' which, to use an American expression, 'sky-rocketed' in the aftermath of World War I and the downfall of the Ottoman Empire. No less significant was the Arab-centered identification of 'non-Arab' with 'non-Muslim', an erroneous misconception which was ignorantly derived from Taymiyya's anti-foreign sentiments. While it began as part of an anti-Mongol and anti-crusades campaign, his aversion for the foreign was later seized by various political movements in the twentieth century for varying causes and purposes, including the moral mobilization against the Western powers as 'crusading' ones. Forever conceived as 'crusading', the Western states were habitually seen as aiming at Islam and its nations as the case was demonstrated clearly during and after the U.S. invasion of Iraq, 2003.

Taymiyya's ruling (*fatwa*) to wage a holy war (*jihad*) against the Mongols set a precedent for the later identification in neo-Islamic ideology of Islamic revivalism with the anti foreign, providing neo-Islamic energies with the much needed political focus and purpose which later neo-Islamic groups required to portray an anti-Western self image to promote their popularity. As such, the neo-Islamic groups met with the pan-Arab movements in a single anti-colonial and then anti-Western (significantly, the USA is mistaken for a colonial power in the Islamic world) discourse which benefited the pan-Arab movements considerably during the twentieth century when the latter movements monopolized state power for decades upholding an Islamic façade to win popularity. This common neo-Islamic and pan-Arab allegedly nationalist drive, however, broke up in later years because of the ideological incompatibility between the two political trends. Yes, they both entertained elusive ancestral dreams of revivalist programs, but were totally different in nature and purpose. A puritanical caliphate of the neo-Islamic vision does not fit squarely into the visions of the Arab nationalist officers or royals currently in power in the Middle East. This incongruity hides behind the certainty of the departure. Once they suspected anti-regime activities administered by the neo-Islamic 'Muslim Brotherhood' (*ikhwan al-Muslimeen*), Egypt's pan-Arab nationalist president Gamal abd al-Nasir and both of his successors, Sadat and Mubarak, launched merciless campaigns to terminate the Brotherhood and persecute its leading cadre.[8] Such breakup incidents in Egypt, Syria, Iraq, Algeria and Yemen, in addition to the alarming and repugnant division between the Saudi royal family and the radical wing of the neo-Islamic Wahabis, all demonstrate the discord between the neo-Islamists and the Arab nationalists, irrespective of their former opportunistic agreement. The alliance of the nationalists (generally in control of state power in the Arab World, thanks to the British made League of Arab States) and the neo-Islamists had a timely purpose because the former regimes used the latter as an anti-dote for communist and leftist propaganda during the Cold War era. This 'abuse' of neo-Islam proved to be a double-edged weapon, particularly in the case of the generous support it obtained from the West to resist the Soviets and force their forces out of Afghanistan before 9/11, with a specific reference to the subsequent dramatic collisions.

Although destined to disintegrate, the above alliance between the two revivalist trends is by no means rootless as it dates back to the early intellectual stirrings of the so-called Arab-Islamic 'renaissance' (*nahdha*) of the nineteenth century, an intellectual awakening which was inspired by simplistic comparisons and contrasts between the backwardness of the Arab and Islamic nations and the progress of the modern European nations.[9] The works of the major renaissance intellectuals, Rifa'a Rafi' al-Tahtawi (1801-1873), Khayr al-Dīn al-Tunisi (1820-1890), Jamal al-Dīn al-Afghani (1838-1897) and Muhammed Abdu (1849-1905) do not seem to distinguish clearly between 'Arab' and 'Muslim". Both were interchangeably used in their relevant political literature, for this matter. It was due to such a cloudy legacy, it went for granted that both qualities were synonymous and commonly used to indicate one referent.

Rooted back in the Umayyad chauvinist legacy, [10] the identification of Arab with Muslim was by no means inconsequential, particularly in so far as the Sunni-Shi'i controversy was concerned. Nonetheless, the issue underwent changes and produced complicated ramifications urged by the anxiety that it might ruin the universality of the faith. Taymiyya partook in creating this confusion as his hatred for foreign coercion was misinterpreted as a pro-Arab bias which would attain a kind of triumphant fulfillment in a Sunni Arab state presided by an Arab caliph. This was behind the popularity among Sunni Arab youth of neo-Islamic ideology in the contemporary Arab World. If we survey neo-Islamic terror groups, we would inevitably notice that they are organized and led by Arabs such as Usama Bin Ladin and his successor, Ayman al-Dhawahiri.

Taymiyya's theoretical foundation produced a set of ideas, theses and goals that kept on combining neo-Islamic groups, with Arab nationalists down to the present day.

IV. Wahabi Neo-Islam:

Wahabism is another significant outgrowth of neo-Islam. As indicated before, neo-Islam began as a response to the eclipse of the Islamic civilization and its Arab controlled caliphate. As a cultural response to such alarming stimuli, neo-Islam was initiated by Taymiyya, a polemicist whose aspirations and visions were taken up by a number of disciples and imitators who were all labeled as 'renovators' who, not only agreed with several of Taymiyya's essential ideas, resumed his polemic and carried it to extremes at times to the extent that some of them radicalized it by modifications and shifts of emphasis to deal more aggressively and violently with the causes of the 'crisis of Islam', to use Bernard Lewis' favorite words, in the modern world. As the dilemma was traced back to the decline of the Islamic, 'Arab' state and the consequent widespread decadence which engulfed the Muslim nations following the Mongol and other barbaric tribes' invasions, Muslims required, say, updated propositions and ideas to withstand the decline and resist stronger and cannier foreign newcomers to the Islamic world. Though mostly critical of it, the Turkish, Ottoman caliphate was tolerably dealt with by later neo-Islamists for being the only remaining Sunni Muslim caliphate that seemed to provide at least a nominal trans-ethnic Islamic nexus (as opposed to the successive rival Shi'i dynasties of Iran). As such neo-Islam deepened and sharpened its divisive Sunni bias, reinforcing the hypothesis that it was the Sunni Muslim response to its own historical failures which had cost it the loss of its monopoly of state power because it succumbed to the erosive currents that had issued from foreign non-Muslim regions. Once Sunni Islam lost its monopoly of state power, a historically phenomenal exchange of roles with the everlasting Shi'i opposition took place. In this case Shi'i Islam handled a double task: on the one hand, it provided the new Sunni opposition with a huge storehouse of mutual grievances; and on the other, it presented operational opposition techniques for anti-government activities. It was, therefore, feasible for the neo-Islamic zealots to retreat to the Shi'i opposition archives within the context of the search for effective tools of protest and methods for destabilizing the state. Hence the obvious similarities between today's Sunni neo-Islamic terrorist organizations and the Shi'i groups that had historically opposed Sunni authorities from the beginning of Umayyad rule. Parallelisms between the ways of the Shi'i 'Order of Assassins', the 'Brethren of Purity' and today's Sunni neo-Islamic tactics are too obvious to pass unnoticed.

Certain of the complexity of the task to revive the spirit of early Islam in a contemporaneous Muslim world already submerged by ignorance, backwardness and frailty, the neo-Islamists thought it their most important task to restore and retain early Islamic austerity and seriousness of purpose as a prerequisite to withstand and defeat the foreign thrust into the Islamic world. Neo-Islamic activists realized that such a far-fetched goal, which involved deracinating deep-rooted habits and alien convictions common among Muslims, could only be realized by the intensive use of the tools of coercion and compulsion for an ignorant and exceedingly sluggish Muslim world which had been made effeminate by the masculine intrusions of the Western industrial states. Apparently swallowed by the high tide of foreign, especially Western, hegemony, the Islamic World needed a tough masculine response to give it a shock of recognition. The deliberate and mandatory employment of such compulsive tools amounted to excommunication and even 'infidelizing' (*takfīr*) of Muslims who do not abide by the strict rules set up by the neo-Islamic zealots. Once made an infidel, a Muslim is dismissed as an outcast and, worse, as an apostate. In both cases, his blood is permissible, if not obligatory, to spill, particularly in the cases of rejecting or criticizing neo-Islamic beliefs, an apparent reminder of the Assassins' dogmatic terror.

It was at this milestone of neo-Islam's development that there appeared an important shift of emphasis and tactic: while neo-Islam had begun with Taymiyya's embittered anti-foreign thrust, focusing mainly on the foreign foe, it refocused its aggressive energies against the 'foe within', mobilizing emphatically against those Muslims who seemed to the neo-Islamists like 'soft targets' which were penetrable by the foreign foe. By the time Taymiyya put down his 'renewal' theory, the Mongol enemy was much more urgent than the intrinsic elements of weakness in the world of Islam, according to his line of thinking. His criticism of Shi'ism and Sufism was milder than the cut-throat Puritanism of the later neo-Islamists, particularly that of the Wahabis, though he set a precedent for much of their extremist elaboration.

Though Taymiyya had turned reform and renovation into the neo-Islam we have surveyed so far, Muhammed ibn abd al-Wahab (1703-1791), (henceforth, Wahab) made the whole renewal discourse a bleak, black-or-white, issue of extremes, turning it puritanical, with a specific reference to over-stressing Islamic monotheism (*tawhīd*) to rid it of what seemed to him alien elements which degraded the doctrine of the oneness of the Godhead. Wahab, therefore, put down a set of strict criteria to sort out what was Islamic and what was not, in a huge and sweeping value-judging campaign. Of course, such a set of criteria was bound to be authoritative and of a compulsory nature. It proved to be so extreme that it ended up by excommunicating, not only the Shi'a and the Sufis,[11] but also all Muslim adherents of the other traditional Sunni schools of jurisprudence[12]: al-Hanafiyya, al-Shafi'yya, al-Malikiyya and al-Hanbaliyya. Passing such harsh judgments on a wholesale manner, it became clear that only Wahabi Muslims were genuine Muslims from Wahab's perspectives. The rest were either 'deifiers' of agents or persons beyond God (*mushrekeen*) or believers in emergent alien practices and accretions (*bidé*) such as the ones that had no proven precedent in early Islam. The Wahabi dismissal of non-Wahabi Muslims as impure went so far as to prefer dealing with the foreign Christians or Jews rather than dealing with the 'sham-Muslims' who follow the other traditional sects. Algar notes this Wahabi bias, stating that "In short, better a Christian than a non-Wahabi Muslim"[13], echoing abd al-Aziz ibn Saud's words addressed to Philby, Britain's ambassador to him as the first king of the dynasty that monopolized state power in the kingdom of 'Saudi' Arabia from that time to the present day.

As Hamid Algar pursues an argument in his treatment of Wahab that leads to deracinating his ideas from the soil of former neo-Islamic revivalist literature, stating that Wahab virtually "came out of nowhere,"[14] justifiably stressing the differences between his and Taymiyya's arguments, Natan J. Delong-Bas, equally justified, traces several of Wahab's ideas to Taymiyya as an early educational diet for the former.[15]

However, it is significant to note that to survey the major hypotheses and arguments of both types of neo-Islamists would inevitably demonstrate that the similarities between the two outweigh the dissimilarities way more than Algar estimates. Taymiyya had surely been among the formative constituents of Wahab's ideas and those of a host of other neo-Islamists, though Wahab proved to be of a more durable fame in the historical and practical sense because a whole puritanical Islamic sect is now commonly ascribed to him (Wahabism), while a whole state is said to formally follow that sect (The Kingdom of Saudi Arabia).

The historical nexus that combines Wahabism to the Saudi royal family is a perplexing one in so far as the status quo in the Middle East and the whole world of Islam is concerned. It is one that constituted the backbone of the kingdom. It had all begun entwined with Wahab's biography which culminated in a historical alliance between him and Muhammed ibn Saud,[16] the chieftain of the Saudi family because both men saw in their alliance (religious-tribal) promising prospects of limitless possibilities since there was a harmony between the former's urge to purify religion and the latter's aspirations for expansion and annexation using religion as an irresistible vehicle. As such, the Saudi chieftain could use Wahab's puritanical arguments as a justification, not only to impose his authority on neighboring areas, but also to portray a self-image of the conscientious protector of the faith and defender of the holiest Islamic sites later on. Yet the alliance between the two men involved self terminating elements due to its coincidental and opportunistic basis. It began with Wahab's banishment into an exile which happened to be the home town of the Saudi family. In the exile he was warmly welcomed, generously hosted by the Saudis and rewarded with a young wife to comfort him.[17] This incident would in no way remove the unmistakable incongruity between the motives and purposes of the two men and between the aspirations of their followers, the austere Wahabis and the tribal Saudis.

To demonstrate the diversity between Wahab and Saud, it is significant to have an idea of the former's worldview which was essentially extremist because, for him, the world fell in two opposing zones with no *medias res* in between: (1) The zone of Islam (*dar al-Islam*) and (2) The zone of infidelity (*dar al-kufr*). The first is the peaceful zone of Muslims, while the second is the zone of the infidels (irrespective of the forms and grades of infidelity). Once a Muslim happens to be in the second zone, he automatically turns into a fighter in a state of perpetual war and vice versa. Two species of leaders are, accordingly, to preside over each zone: the *imām* (literally, leader) rules supreme in the zone of peace, whereas the emīr (literally, prince) is the supreme commander in the zone of war.[18] Because of the contemporaneous overwhelming sense of being in an antagonistic environment, Wahab elaborated on the martial leader (the *emīr*), probably in a self-reflective effort to define his own role for the future. For him, Muslims are destined to be in a perpetual state of war against the infidels, whether non-Muslims or excommunicated Muslims of Wahab's criteria. The latter category includes, in addition to the traditional outcasts, the Shi'is and sufis, almost all non-Wahabi Muslims.

For a strictly puritanical neo-Islamic approach of Wahab's type, with the terms and conditions he had put down to qualify a reliable ruler (*imām*) or a trustworthy military leader (*amīr*), the Saudis are in no way fitting matches. No less significant is the fact that when the Wahabi-Saudi alliance was concluded, both began an irreligious career of plundering and looting neighboring tribes and villages in an effort not only to subjugate them, but also to impose heavy taxes on the population, though it professed the faith of Islam.[19] The Wahabis deemed such unjust wars holy, *jihad*, because they had considered the neighboring Muslims excommunicated for the simple fact that they did not embrace Wahabism. Forced subjugations and annexations of adjacent areas resulted in creating the nucleus of a political entity led by the ultimate beneficiary of the alliance, the Saudi family.

Although the above alliance continued intact for decades (with occasional disagreements), it is destined to crack one day due to divisive issues that cannot be easily reconciled, with a particular reference to the Wahabi objection to the Saudi family's alliance with, and reliance on Western powers, a situation that made a Wahabi terrorists like Usama Bin Ladin and others dissent and look for direct superheated fronts that would enable them to 'fight' the West beyond the intervention by Saudi authorities. That was how Afghanistan turned into a base and a front for terrorist activities. This dissent should not mean that the decades-old alliance was over as the Wahabi sect is still prevalent in the Saudi kingdom with the traditional Wahabi clerics representing a 'double' government which is capable of practicing checks and controls over the king's executive government.

The Saudi royal family is ever aware that Wahabism

is the backbone of the state. It, therefore, maintains and fosters the old alliance by flattering and catering to the traditional moderate Wahabi clerics who could play a decisive social role inside the kingdom, despite the grievances and the recurrent incidents of rebellion that the extremist Wahabis stage occasionally. The Saudi family has to maintain the difficult balance between the internal alliance with the Wahabis and the external alliance with the West, particularly with the USA. It is this sensitive and liquid tie between the royals and the Wahabis in Saudi Arabia which is apt to create problems in the future. Today, one may note two types of Wahabis. Firstly, the 'high' Wahabis represented by the privileged pro-Saudi clerics who have the upper hand in controlling the society and administrating the holiest sites of Islam, in addition to education and the media, among other vital sectors, using their infamous compulsive apparatus of the religious police, better known as *al-mutaween*.[20] And secondly, the 'low' Wahabis represented by the impoverished extremist zealots who reject the alliance and, therefore, head to such fronts in the zone of war as Afghanistan, Pakistan, Syria and Iraq, among other superheated regions to partake in the 'grand jihad' of neo-Islam against those who seem to them as the masked crusaders of our time. While the high Wahabis make privileged elite which benefits from its Saudi patrons, the low Wahabis have no benefactors other than the religious enthusiasts or the rich dissenters like Bin Laden. They are the 'proletarian' Wahabis, if the term is permissible in this context, who sacrifice themselves in anticipation of an instant transfer from the earthly bloody battlefield to the heavenly paradise where they expect to live with angelic women (*hūr al'eyn*) in everlasting happiness.

As the equilibrium is difficult to maintain endlessly by the Saudi royal family, and because the incongruent foreign alliances may pose existential threat to it, the whole complexity becomes a matter of choice: which of the alliances the Saudis have to embrace to keep their authority. This problem hides behind the divisions inside the royal family, between the pro-West liners and the pro-Wahabi conservatives. The conflict is brewing and is apt to break out as one of the trends must prevail.

Chapter IV

The Two Potentials of Neo-Islam:
The Muslim Brotherhood

The Muslim Brotherhood may be conceived as a relatively moderate reformulation of neo-Islamic principles since it rejects a number of Taymiyya's hypotheses and replaces Wahabi exclusive extremism by a tolerant broad pan-Islamic theory that, though essentially Sunni embraces a vision of combining all Muslims together, irrespective of sectarian variants and jurisprudent differences. Though moderate, some of its members have frequently slipped into Wahabi extremism in times of turmoil and political protest, particularly on occasions when the Brotherhood's moderate tendency is met by governmental short-sighted coercion which is usually coupled with compulsive measures meant to repress or terminate it. Hence the frequent dissent of several of the Brotherhood's disillusioned members in favor of more radical, even terrorist, brands of neo-Islam, including several of the current members of *al-Qa'ida* and of similar terror groups. In this instance, the liquid boundaries among the various versions of neo-Islamic groups merge and overlap, each with a program and a vision of its own. Yet, the jarring variants rely on a unifying set of motives and goals which were put down by former neo-Islamists like Taymiyya, encompassing all of the neo-Islamic groups within a single framework.

Note, for an instance, the Brotherhood's commitment to the revelation (*Qur'ān*) and the traditions of the prophet (*Sunna*) as the sole referential sources for Islamic life and work.[1] Both serve as the ultimate sources of the Islamic law (*shari'a*) which is the ultimate aspiration of neo-Islamic groups to organize the future Islamic utopian society and state. Once a neo-Islamic individual or a group mentions the word 'state', it automatically, suggests the envisaged 'model' state that follows in the footsteps of the afore-mentioned four orthodox caliphs whose state was by no means fault-free.[2] In this aspiration, the Brotherhood does not fare far from Taymiyya's broad guidelines and, of course, Wahabism's puritanical austerity, though it does from its medieval forerunner, the Brethren of Purity (See: chapter II, above).

Although it avowedly declares its commitment to democracy and to political work as civility, the Muslim Brotherhood seems to consider such Western political traditions only as timely vehicles for a purpose, to realize the Islamic caliphate, a vision that frequently surfaces in its writers' literature which eventually externalizes another one of its distinctive neo-Islamic tenets, its low opinion of the Western World and its antipathy to its policies, particularly in the Middle East. When one surveys the Muslim Brotherhood's history in its birthplace, Egypt, and elsewhere (being a global Islamic organization), he is bound to conclude that its declared commitment to

Western political traditions and practices is tactical and relatively temporary, particularly when its members, the 'Brothers', feel that democracy, for instance, can be abused and betrayed by political rivals for opportunistic and unprincipled purposes such as distancing the Brotherhood from authority. When Egypt's ex-president, Muhammed Morsi (a leading member of the Brotherhood) was deposed and imprisoned by the army after a single year in power (2013) as the first democratically elected president in the whole history of Egypt, the Muslim Brothers took to the streets of Cairo and the other major Egyptian cities in protest, bitterly protesting the failure of their democratic vision which proved to have been only a dramatic performance of a farce that ended up mirroring, not the will of the people, the will of other political performers, domestic, regional and foreign, performers who were capable of twisting democracy into totalitarianism when the former exceeds certain limits. Alarmingly, the Muslim Brothers discredited and discarded the Egyptian version of democracy which had proven to be a false parade. As such, it would implicitly follow that they should feel free-handed to adopt any method possible to restore state power to its 'legitimate' winners. This is exactly why the post-Morsi turmoil, if it continues unresolved, could be of incalculable destructive consequences in a heated cauldron over-charged with the demonic energies of a major Middle-Eastern country with a population of about 92,000,000 consisting mostly of Muslim impoverished and discontented citizens. The danger of radicalizing the erstwhile peaceful Muslim Brotherhood is, therefore, imminent and threatening to destabilize the whole region by the probable wholesale recruitment of the Brotherhood's millions of adherents in terror groups, exactly like what happened when its former disillusioned dissenters turned to terror in Algeria and elsewhere. Such a grim scenario would apparently exhibit the afore-mentioned liquid boundaries among the neo-Islamic groups, particularly when the failure of democracy justified terror.

No less indicative of this alarming situation are the various façades the Muslim Brotherhood and other neo-Islamic groups use as curtains to hide behind. The Muslim Brotherhood did make such organs in disguise to define and modify its political and social role from time to time and in accordance with the locations of its activities. In addition to the 'Muslim Sisters' organ, it created several political parties that joined in the 'meal of democracy' when and wherever such reformulations were possible or necessary. The Muslim Brotherhood's political organ in Egypt took the title of the 'Freedom and Justice Party', whereas in Iraq it preferred the title of the 'Islamic Party'. It appeared in Gaza and the West Bank under the name of *Hamas,*[3] in addition to other organs in Turkey, Pakistan and Tunisia among other countries. More demonstrative of the risks of discarding the 'democratic way' to attain power in favor of the 'activist way' are the groups that had broken away from The Muslim Brotherhood to run a more fundamentalist course as was the case with the 'Islamic Liberation Party' (*hizb al-tahrīr al-islami*), the Islamic group (*al-jama'a al-islamiyya*) and the extremist 'Infidelizing and Migration Group' (*al-takfir wal Hijra*) which had assassinated Egypt's former president, Anwar al-Sadāt, and temporarily hosted Ayman al-Dhawahiri (the first man in *al-Qa'ida* currently) prior to joining Bin Ladin's 'The Base'. Breakaway groups from the Brotherhood have all settled in the category of terror, indicating the alarming possibilities of its possible swift shift to the same militant camp.

Another of the traits that the Muslim Brotherhood shares with other neo-Islamic groups is its obsession with the ancestral dream, not only that of establishing a caliphate, but also of extending it into an 'Empire of Neo-Islamic Virtue', an empire which has, as its formative prerequisites, the defeat of the materialistic empires of the 'imperial' West and the consequent spread of Islam (the seal of all revealed religions) throughout the globe. The caliphate seems to be only a stepping-stone to a universal state which complements the unfinished work of the historical one.

Note the themes of continuity and resumption of what was accomplished in history before. Not only was the 'caliphate' theme inspired by the power vacuum which the fall of the Ottoman caliphate had created, it was also inspired by a vision of transcontinental 'world state' of the united Islamic nations. As Hasan al-Banna, the founder of the Islamic Brotherhood, visualized it, the caliphate was to expand as wide as the former Islamic world of the Middle Ages, from the Iberian Peninsula (Spain and Portugal) to the Far East (Indonesia).[5]

Such an endeavor is bound to involve a struggle that culminates into a holy war (*jihad*) for the fulfillment of its target, even when *jihad* requires the ultimate sacrifice of a neo-Muslim's life. Nowhere are the tenets of the Muslim Brotherhood more apparently stated than in its central slogan: "*Allah* is our objective, the *Qura'ān* is our law, the prophet is our leader, *jihad* is our way and death for Allah's sake is the ultimate of our aspirations" (translation mine).

In line with Wahabi antipathy to those Muslims whom

the Wahabis had excommunicated, Sayed Qutb, the most outspoken writer of the Muslim Brotherhood, wished to launch a purification campaign to rid the Islamic 'nation' (*umma*) of what he called 'the internal enemy', that enemy which seemed to him to forerun a rebirth of the flaws of the 'age of ignorance' (*jahiliyya*) which Islam had eradicated, allegedly, for good. Another age of ignorance was imminent and rapidly approaching, according to Qutb. It had to be withstood. His fear of such an inevitable dark age was actually inspired by his observation of the Muslims' blind thrust to imitate the West, particularly American life and culture.

One should blame this criticism on his stay in the USA and his revulsion from the concurrent wide spread anti-Muslim and anti-Arab sentiments there, coinciding with the mounting tensions between the Arabs and the Israelis that which stimulated him to denounce American policies and, by way of causation, the American way of life. They were the Arab-Israeli wars that originally instigated his critique of American society, a critique which ranges from attacking its blind and blinding materialism, that which had made "churches . . . operate like businesses", [6] and turned the houses of worship into theaters of "sexual promiscuity".[7] This opinion could shed light on the Brotherhood's perplexing double-faceted attitude to the Western World and its political and economic models. No less significant in this respect were the suspicions the Brotherhood continually maintained and fostered concerning the Western states' support for Israel during its wars with the neighboring Arab states. The Brotherhood took a stance that supported the Arab states and fuelled mass sentiments against Israel.

Yet, the Muslim Brotherhood promoted a moderate and civil concept of evolutionary, not revolutionary change, a commendable concept that it had distillated out of its non-stop suffering under the successive totalitarian regimes which took control in Egypt, royal and republican. This kind of continual suppression, coupled by the religious appeal for a traditional society could have been among the major causes behind the popularity of the Muslim Brotherhood which handled a strong mobilizing role during the dramatic events of the so-called 'Arab Spring', forcing the last of the military presidents, Hosni Mubarak, to resign in 2011. Egypt's first democratic elections of 2012 verified the huge popularity of the Muslim Brotherhood which achieved an overwhelming parliamentary majority that enabled it to nominate the president. The erstwhile imprisoned Muhammed Morsi (who had studied in the USA) suddenly became the first elected leader of Egypt in history. Though destined to be short-lived (only one year) Morsi's presidency proved beyond doubt that Egypt was still the prey of the powerful officer corps which had succeeded to keep civil peace during the superheated events of the so-called 'revolution' (2011), the following elections (2012) and then during the turmoil and instability which arose from the army's ousting of Morsi by an unexpected maneuver. Democracy could not survive with a strong army in the states of the Middle East, to be sure.

Though ousting Morsi produced much backfire as the democracy-betrayed supporters of the Muslim Brotherhood kept on staging protest and threatening 'action' to restore legitimacy and install Morsi as the president again, there is ample evidence that the Brotherhood is willing to check and control its supporters' grievances and protests against the failure of the civil devolution of power within a peaceful framework of civil political change. This tendency stems from the fact that the Brotherhood began as a charitable society aiming to promote the Islamic identity, morality and prosperity wherever Muslims lived. It was a peaceful tendency that might have grown out of the Brotherhood's global aspirations which were supported by organs reaching out to the scattered Muslim minorities as far as the Fiji Islands,[8] a situation that tempered the radical sentiments down. The global tenet might account for the Muslim Brotherhood's frequently marked mild brand of neo-Islamism. Its founder, Hasan al-Banna, seemed to have been aware of the global aspirations of his group right from the beginning in1928, forecasting its pan-Islamic dimension as a neo-Islamic project. He stated the obvious about the faith of Islam to serve the group's universal ambitions, stating that "Islam does not recognize geographical boundaries, nor does it acknowledge national and blood differences, considering all Muslims as one *umma*".[9] The geographical breadth of the Brotherhood's neo-Islamic social and political action made it necessary to take the pan-Islamic tolerant course of persuasion, not violence, to avoid ruthless suppression in foreign lands especially where Muslims appeared to be powerless minorities. As such, it clang to a distinctive global neo-Islamic vision of reviving a world 'caliphate' in the aftermath of the reverberating fall of the Ottoman Empire, last of the caliphates. He once addressed a number of the Brotherhood congregants, urging them to "elect a new Caliph, replacing the Ottoman ruler whose downfall Europe engineered".[10] Loaded with anti-European sentiments, this invitation for the Brothers to respond by establishing a global neo-Islamic state[11] should be put against a background of domestic politics mostly steered by Egyptian politicians who were bewitched by the idea of imitating the European states and following into their footsteps to attain a degree of local progress. As the anti-West tenet of the Brotherhood continued unabated from the monarchy to the Egyptian 'Free Officers' republic, it was misconceived by the state as an obstacle to progress.

This could shed light on the unrelenting suppression the Brotherhood had suffered in republican Egypt right from 1952 to 2011 when the last of the officers was forced to resign from the presidency. For such consecutive regimes the Brotherhood's neo-Islamic project sounded essentially regressive, particularly for President Naser whose pan-Arab socialistic program had been on the run. Consequently, accumulative persecution and suppression seemed to have tamed the impulsive and violent potential that dwelled deep in the Brotherhood in line with most of the neo-Islamic groups. When the Muslim Brothers went to the polls to elect a president, hopefully from their ranks, they were all optimism and trust that genuine democracy, as a touchstone, was bound to unravel their wide influence and popularity among the Egyptian people. To depose the first and, probably, last Muslim Brotherhood president, Muhammed Morsi, a year later was surely a violent shock of recognition for the leading cadre of the Brotherhood as it made it realize the unbridgeable gap which extends between the society and the neo-Islamic program. For them, it was a tragic failure of vision which is expected to dig deep into the neo-Islamic psyche to make it feel that it is engulfed by ruthless domestic and regional international opponents who would not tolerate any form of a neo-Islamic regime.

Yet, and as pointed above, the Muslim Brotherhood still retains and maintains a potential fundamental tendency that can turn terrorist when betrayed by democracy and deprived of its fruits, as was the situation in Algeria in the early years of the 1990's. The current stirrings and civil unrest which the Brotherhood stages in protest against the removal of Morsi by the military, in addition to the

Sinai *salafia* confrontations with the army may prefigure a 'Bin Ladin pattern' of dissent in favor of terror. Such a probability is imminent because Bin Ladin had already accused the Muslim Brotherhood of "diluting the Islamist agenda so as to sooth Western fears".[12] Staunch advocates of terror like Bin Ladin and his successor in *al-Qa'ida*, Ayman al-Dhawahiri, conceived the Brotherhood's moderation and approval of a West-friendly involvement in democracy as treason to the ongoing holy war and betrayal of the ideological foundation which had been put down by the famous ideologue, Sayed Qutb.[13]

Loyal to its original purpose as a charitable society which is reliant for its finances on the members' donations, the Muslim Brotherhood's tinge of fundamentalism may endure potent, though static for some time till it turns active and liberate limitless demonic energies destructively. This is exactly what must be alarming in the Egyptian situation and in its expected echoes from fellow Brothers in various parts of the world. Note especially Turkey's Islamic Prime

Minister's, Recep Tayyib Erdoğan, denunciation of the Egyptian army's unexpected move of ousting Morsi and his public rejection of sending him to the court of law. For Erdogan, this was a blunt breach of democracy and of the constitutionality of Morsi's presidency.

Financially independent, the Muslim Brotherhood preserves and cherishes a political freedom that keeps it beyond external influences. This financial independence, combined with its charitable purposes, has continually urged the moneyed elite of its members to enhance their private sector endeavor to accumulate more and more wealth within the supportive free-market environment of the post-Naser presidency. There is no objection from the Brotherhood against individual economic enterprises since they are partly channeled for the Brotherhood's organizational purposes and partly for the charitable ones. Charity is mistaken for partisan political work. In an overpopulated country with chronic poverty problems such moneys can define a notably significant social, not to say political, role particularly when they are given to help the impoverished and the needy through the mosque, not the state. This politically consequential tenet has practically resulted in the growth of several millionaires from the Brotherhood's ranks. Suzy Hansen of *The Economist* deals with this phenomenon favorably in the hope of developing a "leadership core" consisting of "neo-liberals".[14]

In spite of the fact that the similarities between the Muslim Brotherhood's principles and those of other neo-Islamic groups, like those of the Wahabis, are too obvious to pass unnoticed (significantly, the Egyptian Muslim Brothers used to prefer the Saudi, Wahabi, exile to others for such similarities), it is crucial to encourage and enhance those dissimilarities it retains to foster its moderation, lest the more radical neo-Islamic elements inside it should win the moderate portion of the Brotherhood's leadership to a course of violence which distances it from the civil practice of politics, keeping in mind that the terrorist groups are ascending the staircase of neo-Islamic politics rapidly in the current period. Such a policy should both be careful and cautious, particularly after the threats to resort to terror by several of its disillusioned members in the media channels after Morsi had been 'kidnapped' by the 'coup' executers and put in prison, leaving the presidency for a temporary presidency installed by the army Generals.

The Egyptian Muslim Brotherhood is presently in an alarming and shaky position of indecision, torn between its pro-democracy members and its more radical elements that have been painfully embittered by the failure of the vision of democracy in Egypt's first democratic experience. As the incongruity between the pro-Morsi presidency and the army's will continues to shed doubt on the outcomes of democracy in the Islamic countries, it would be quite probable that this multi-million member Muslim Brotherhood would undergo a split between its moderate pro-democracy members and its hardliners. Once such a split takes place, Egypt and the whole Sunni-majority Muslim world would be in serious danger as the huge membership of the Brotherhood might splinter into tens, or more, of violent bands consisting of sub-groups which, betrayed by the failure of the vision of democracy, might engage in armed struggle to fulfill neo-Islam's goals.

Chapter V

Feminizing the West

The argument of this work is bound to lead to a conclusion which, simply stated, indicates that neo-Islam is essentially an internal issue that has to do with the Islamic World or, at least, with the Muslim jurists for their alleged role as custodians of the faith and the 'authorized' spiritual leaders of the faithful. Initially, one must tackle the status quo in the Islamic World through the perplexing question: does Islam have a problem with the Western World to justify the neo-Islamic war against the Western states, societies and civilizations? And, how can the animosity of neo-Islam to the West be relevant to the xenophobia that constituted the neo-Islamic discourse and attitudes ever since Taymiyya laid the retrospective and nostalgic basis of his self-assigned errand to 'renew' or 'regenerate' early Islam within the framework of an obsessive ancestral dream. Aspiring to verify the cyclical movement of history by seeking (at times, making up) patterns of recurrence, neo-Islam develops a persuasive discourse which, based on the past, caters to a motivating future vision which, though nebulous, to be realized by the faithful no matter at what price, including one's own life, of course.

It is here that the historical lesson became crucial to the neo-Islamic revivalist frame of mind, purposely preparing, in retrospect, the way Prophet Muhammed was compelled to militancy by necessity, exchanging persuasion by force, the word by the sword for the spread of Islam. Firstly, he dealt mildly with the internal enemy which consisted of his fellow citizens and, as a great spiritual teacher, he called on them to discard praying for the mute idols that had been made of stone or wood, to worship, Allah, a God Who could not be seen. Defying the heart of the town's economy (the idols), he told everybody that no idol can be divine or an auxiliary vehicle to the Deity. But failing to persuade the idolatrous and the polytheists to embrace a strictly monotheistic faith, Muhammed acknowledged defeat by running away with his small group of the early disciples (known as the companions of the messenger of God) in search of a refuge in an exile, Medina. This historical shift from home to exile was so decisive in the history of Islam that it was taken by the Muslims as the zero year of the Islamic lunar calendar (the *Hijra*, meaning the year of immigration). It created an enemy to fight simply by changing positions, now being outside Mecca where the immigrants had left their properties and their loved ones to save their souls. An enemy was an important motivating and militarizing factor to help vent out this minority group's psychological wrathful pressure by making a vengeful force which sought retaliation against their erstwhile 'cousins' and fellow citizens. But such a mold of tribal and urban ties no more mattered to the few Muslims whom Muhammed had taught to be a single new community (*umma*) with ties that transcended the old bonds of kinship, race, color and class. Prophet Muhammed made everyone of his disciples believe that the Muslims had undergone a rebirth and a new baptism into a new 'nation' unified, for the first time in the history Arabia, by a single faith. To alleviate his disciples' bitterness at being forced out of their home town, empty-handed, to seek refuge in an alien town, he made a clever arrangement to overcome their problem by a 'fraternizing' process (*mu'akhat)*, making everyone of them share (half by half) the properties of those who had invited the refugees to come to their town, Medina. The hosts originally belonged to two tribes[1] and were honored by the title of 'the supporters' (*al-annsār*) because they voluntarily supported the cause of Islam and provided asylum to its powerless adherents. This 'fraternizing' process between the refugees and the town citizens is surely a great achievement that is ascribed to the potential power of a new religious nexus. This should have been the source of the theme of the Islamic brotherhood. According to some Muslims, Muhammed had forerun Karl

Marx and other socialists by that early commonwealth. But from another perspective, one might ascribe the town's enthusiastic support for the new faith, and its readiness to make such sacrifices to host a fugitive minority to a strong desire to replace Mecca as a pilgrimage site by their own town with the help of the new religion, fixing an eye on the economic benefits expected from such a shift in the pilgrimage center which attracted the Arabs annually for worship, trading and verbal fencing.[2]

Historically, this was not a new attempt to disarm Mecca of its religious and economic privileges as a center of pilgrimage. The envied town had been challenged by an Abyssinian king, named Ebraha, who tried to redirect the pilgrims from Mecca to a site he had chosen, a situation which indicated the rivalries among the towns to be the pilgrimage focus of the adherents of the various religious systems. It had an economic dimension, to be sure. This could shed light on the Medinans' enthusiasm for the new religion of Islam.

The repositioning of the small refugee community of the early Muslims turned everything upside down, especially with reference to political power balances. The important development took place when that nascent community, loaded by vengeful sentiments against its former suppressors, made up a 'foreign foe' of them. It so followed that the formerly aggressive fellow citizens who had the upper hand, were confronted by the sword, having failed to comprehend the erstwhile peaceful 'message' by the coldness of the word

Because the refuge town was not only home of the two supportive tribes that had originally embraced Islam and offered Muhammed and his disciples an asylum and fraternized them, the rest of the citizens who declined to embrace Islam provided another foreign enemy for the already wrathful refugee Muslims. Muhammed categorized the rest of the citizens either as Jews (*yehud*), who were fellow monotheists, or hypocrites (*munafiqeen*), those who pretended to profess Islam, to escape the wrath of the, now, powerful Muslim refugees.

Enemies in the history of Islam were not hard to make, particularly with the conceptualization of the 'idol', expanding its meaning from the tangible object which used to be worshipped before to practically anything, ruler, concept or morality that eventually serves an identical idolatrous purpose reminding of the original idol. Idolatry, accordingly, included wealth, race, class, color and gender, among other things.[3]

The pitiless enemy had forced militarization on Islam in the post-Meccan period, giving birth to a militant Islam that achieved considerable victories in the field during a relatively short duration of time. Subject to a vengeful and aggressive drive, and terrified by the sense of being surrounded by enemies of varying goals, the new militant Islam sought refuge in violent, sometimes ruthless, responses to the enemies around it, impulsive responses that used the utmost force to defeat the enemies, at times, mercilessly. In short, the Muslims decided to be a masculine power which initiates confrontations rather than of receives its impact passively.

Within its basically revivalist discourse, neo-Islam aspires to run the above-summarized historical course once again, disregarding the great time span (about fourteen centuries) that expands between the reported past and the novel present, including all the changes that took place throughout. This may be one of the most retarding flaws of neo-Islam as it reads the past into the present to obtain guidelines for the present and the future. In fact it lives in the dust-gathering historical narrative in search of a key that can help it decipher the incomprehensible and problematic present and redress it, accordingly.

The above-mentioned historical narrative concerning the militarization of Islam seems to have captivated the imagination of the extremist groups of contemporary neo-Islam as an inspiration and justification for terror as has been the case with *al-Qa'ida* and its offshoots such as

today's active ISIS (The Islamic State of Iraq and Syria).
The discourse such terror groups adopted in addressing
the Western World (considered synonymous with idolatry,
according to the neo-Islamic conception) is basically
authoritative and it smacks of an unmistakable vengeful
drive. It, therefore, sounds shocking to the Western
World because its language conveys an obvious air of
authority that is meant to undermine Western hegemony
by 'feminizing' it. In its threats, terms, deadlines and even
'advices' (best illustrated by inviting the Western nations
to embrace Islam in a wholesale manner), the discourse
of such groups echoes the historical narrative of the early
Muslims who turned powerful by migration (*hijra*). Hence
the thrust by thousands of migrants from various parts of
the world to the superheated war zones to partake in the
'grand' *jihad* wars in Syria, Afghanistan, Iraq or elsewhere.
It is seen as following in the footsteps of the prophet and
his companions, migration matters in such situations. In
a televised speech Usama bin Ladin made the above case

of authority obvious as he had once made sure to address the American people like a different entity from the U.S. administration in an appeal to 'befriend' the former and confuse the latter to cause a division. Yet, the authoritative language amounted to the point that the *al-Qa'ida* speaker threatened the American people with dire consequences if it did not listen and resist the administration's evil deeds and 'schemes' against the Muslims. With a specific reference to the historical narrative, immigration provides the immigrants with the strength and steadfastness they lacked at home before.

It is significant to note that this kind of language is virtually a reversal of the colonial discourse that stuck to the Western World (the U.S. included), having been established by the early decades of the European age of empire-building and reiterated by Cold War decades. The reversal is stressed by terrorist neo-Islam to exhibit an opposite Muslim World, no more the veiled weakened, submissive and deferential feminine entity of the golden age of European colonialism. It is significant to note that, though never involved in colonialism, the U.S. is usually included in the anti-West campaign simply because of the neo-Islamic conception of the whole West as a Christian 'crusading' power, a residual remnant from Taymiyya's identification of the foreign with the anti-Muslim, and of both with decadence. The implication is not far-fetched to grasp: the shared responsibility of all Western powers in all the problems that inflict the Muslim World. The crusades are once again recalled from the medieval past to be applied to the present, allegedly, for clearer perspectives and comprehensible conclusions, according to the neo-Islamic line of thinking. Several of the American journalists who rushed into Iraq during or after the 2003 US invasion were literally 'shocked' when some Iraqis expressed their rejection of 'American colonialism'! Echoing the Cold War era and the concurrent communist and pan-Arab rhetoric when such distortive expressions like 'U.S. imperialism' and 'U.S. colonialism' became common among the people who interpreted the 2003 'military invasion' of Iraq in terms of a colonial annexation and expansion, recalling the British invasion of Iraq early in the twentieth century. In the Saddam Hussein period, the fusion of the U.S. with European colonialism was established and enhanced by the media machine which had innovated the 'Anglo-Saxon' nexus to combine the U.S. with Britain and other Anglo-Saxon nations and insert them into a single anti-Iraq and anti-Islam category. Because the neo-Islamist conception of the U.S. as no more than an extension of European colonialism, the distinction between the two becomes difficult to pursue within the Muslim mind which is made to dwell on parallelisms and, to it, meaningful binaries and similarities, thanks to the survival and revival of the 'motifs' of the 'crusades'. According to the neo-Islamic argument, American policies in the Islamic World are old wine in new bottles compared to the European colonial ones. The basic conflict is one, though different are the denominations, according to this dogmatic line of thinking. The yardstick is single: the West' support to Israel.

On the basis of what happened in the historical narrative when Islam turned militant after the migration, the neo-Islamists desire to close the chapter of passive submission to open a new chapter of an aggressive, masculine Islam which is capable of retaliation. The heartless cruelty they deliberately show and purposefully propagate in their dealings with women in any Islamic society they happen to control or effectively influence is, in a way, inspired by the notion that the Western World kept on conceiving the Muslim World as a frail feminine entity,[4] an essentially powerless and passive entity inviting the masculine intrusion of the industrial West. Neo-Islamists see it one of the regrettable moments of history when the frailty of the Muslim societies made it possible for the Western powers to take advantage of their powerlessness to surprise it and enact the domination of male power on female frailty in line with Hegel's *Philosophy of History* "in which the West as subject defeats the East as object in the battle for world-historical ascendency"[5]. Frailty is identified with women and is, therefore, hateful and punishable according to the neo-Islamic psyche since it serves as a reminder of the feminized Muslim space that was 'used', not to say raped, by Western colonialism for too long. According to neo-Islamic rhetoric, such a historical coincidence must not be permitted to recur.

Not only must the weakness be averted, it must be turned upside down this time. It is time to initiate a revivification of the principle of the early Islamic conquests which took the old world by surprise and subjugated the ancient arrogant empires which had a low opinion of the Arabs and Islam. It is supposedly a recurrent historical pattern to be aspired to, and worked for when the horror which the early Muslim conquerors had engendered in neighboring empires was so abrupt and overwhelming that they cracked and disintegrated rapidly leaving the doors wide open for the Muslim thrust to make such nations embrace the faith of Islam that had travelled with the dark manly camel-drivers, ushering intolerably from the wilderness of Arabia.

The neo-Islamic revivalist theory is essentially based on an elective idealization of a certain historical experience (that of the prophet and his four orthodox successors). As this experience is basically one of a militant Islam, it implies the necessity of a reversal of the masculine-feminine exchanges for the modern colonial and postcolonial discourse which saw the masculine industrial West 'invade' and 'use' the feminine Muslim World to fulfill the former's instinctive desires. Neo-Islam means to show that this exploitation should in no way continue or go unpunished; and that the way to put an end to it rests in rejuvenating the coercive masculinity of the spirit of the golden age of the Islamic conquests as an antidote to Western exploitation. The ultimate implication is, therefore, a reversal of roles in the conflict of the universal drama. This purpose is unrealizable according to the neo-Islamic line of thinking without 'shocking' the already 'weakened' Western World by launching unexpected 'incursions' of excessive violence to force the West reconsider its calculations in so far as its attitude to the Muslim nations is concerned.

The obsessive idea is that of terrifying the Western nations to work a psychological invasion consisting of continual fear and horror. The tactic is simple, to be sure: targeting the soft, feminine lacuna in a Western World which is seen by neo-Islamists as weakened and overwhelmed by social, economic and ethical internal problems that originally arose from a spiritual crisis of disbelief. Such soft spots in the Western civilization are not difficult to locate or reach. Most apparent and painful among them is the dependence of the West's capitalist economy on oil, a vital element that is largely held by Muslim nations. This soft spot has recurrently been pointed out by the public speeches of the *al-Qa'ida* leaders, including Bin Ladin who frequently called on the organization operatives, particularly in the oil-rich countries of the Gulf to target the oil fields, pipelines and installations (refineries, ports and tankers), the elements of the masculinity hormone that caters to the West's vital institutions, the industries, the banks and the military machine.

More significant among the weak organs of the West are its allies in the Islamic World, those regimes and regional organizations which are conceived by the neo-Islamists as no more than puppets, especially those whose survival relies on oil revenues which depend on bartering oil for the dollar that rules supreme in the oil-rich countries. Not only do such puppet regimes assist in the West's campaign against neo-Islam, they also sustain a constant supply of oil, using its revenues unwisely to further support Western hegemony.

The commitment the neo-Islamic mentality frequently parades for the dictum of the 'Eye for an eye' mirrors that most alarming and vengeful urge to retaliate by the selfsame coercive methods that the Western World employed ruthlessly to conquer and impose its authority on the Islamic nations. The subsequent radical discourse lays much emphasis, not on the 'feminized' agent-regimes, on what appears to the neo-Islamic eye a number of soft spots 'within' Western civilization such as the moral and spiritual flaws that keep on surfacing on the skin of that civilization, including the widespread family breakdown, homosexuality, drugs and alcoholism, among other deplorable flaws which arise from visceral maladies. Such ominous 'signs of the times' are particularly seized by the neo-Islamic discourse as forerunners of a gloomy fate.

The neo-Islamic ideal of imposing masculinity in its dealing with the West is interrelated to the age-old low opinion of women in the Islamic societies, that opinion which considers women as no more than subservient individuals, ever destined to cater to the compulsive will of the wrathful, dark Muslim man whether a father, brother, husband or son. This dispiriting opinion of womanhood manifests itself rather shockingly in the *jihad* fronts where enthusiastic neo-Muslim women would willingly go and pay their share in the holy wars of neo-Islam by handling the male *jihadists'* sexual needs. Thus the neo-Islamic mentality has innovated a brand of neo-Islamic prostitution, the so-called *'jihad* copulation' (*jihad al-munakaha*) which is said to have been practiced intensively in the Syrian civil war by women who 'migrated' from the various parts of the world, black, blond and Asian. This case has been made public in the Tunisian parliament by the end of 2013 when some of the disgraced male parliament members sounded their objections loudly to the government's laxity in permitting unescorted young women to travel abroad freely. The destinations for such lustful veiled beauties have proved to be the superheated regions where *jihad* was obligatory to neo-Muslims, irrespective of sex, color and marital status. It seems to be hypnotic: virgins and married women combine 'forces' to dedicate themselves to the 'holy' cause voluntarily! On the opposite extreme of such religiously blessed copulations, a woman of light virtue who is caught in a sexual act outside the marriage institution is considered by neo-Islamists adulterous and, therefore, deserving of the *shari'a* verdict of being stoned in public pitilessly. Remember the documentary *Death of a Princes*.

For the neo-Islamic frame of mind, authority is synonymous with masculinity and frailty with femininity, a situation which implies that the former is justified in doing whatever is necessary to impose his will to protect the latter from temptations. A careful examination of the neo-Islamic pursuit of terror would uncover a gender polemic that grew and developed deep inside the neo-Islamic psyche which had derived it from the pre-Islamic dry desert culture for a rebellious ethos that aimed at reversing the masculine-feminine power play of the colonial discourse. This discourse could be traced back to General Napoleon Bonaparte's imposition of his sexuality on the young powerless Egyptian, Fatima, as an emblematic act representing his authority on Egypt through his possession of Fatima's warm and submissive body, though he complained of her smell. It was this same motor that pressed on the British officers in India to play the hero and forbid the Hindu practice of widow voluntary self-cremation (*suttee*) after losing her husband. The purpose, of course, was meant by both the British and the French to propagate a self-image of the blond powerful male protecting the powerless dark Indian female. The terrorist brands of neo-Islam wish to take up this painful colonial legacy to equate terror with masculinity in an attempt to give the Western mind a shock of recognition that would force it review and give up its 'arrogance' and give in to neo-Islamic vision.

Conclusion

To verify the basic hypothesis of this research which is, simply put, that neo-Islam is not Islam, a retreat to the historical narrative of Islam has been methodologically feasible, not to follow in the footsteps of the neo-Islamists who mistook religion for history and vice versa, but to indicate that neo-Islam suffers from the flaw of being essentially imitative and, worse, selective in its appeal to the vestigial past and to 'orthodox' religion as misconceived by its 'renewal' sham-prophets. Such 'prophets' gave themselves the liberty to dwell at length on a seemingly heroic militant phase of a bygone historical phase, a phase which could in no way undergo a resurrection, given the duration of time and the radical changes and developments that took place between the idealized past and the decadent present. Selectivity led to over-looking the chronologically earlier and the religiously purer phase of the Islamic narrative which had begun with the original tenet of a religion that derived its very name from the Arabic word *salām,* meaning peace. The obsessive ancestral dream set the neo-Islamic frame of mind on a dead-ended imitative track which capitalized on a cyclical theory of history and disregarded the fact that Islam is a spiritual tradition, a religion and, by necessity of its reliance on a revelation, is beyond the impact of the passage of time. Religions are supposed to be timeless because they transcend the time dimension. Revelations are beyond human reason because they deal with the absolute Truth, not with the day-to-day facts. In its selectivity, the neo-Islamic theory exceeds its limits and tampers with the zone of the divine, forgetting its theorists' earth-bound sphere.

As neo-Islam is based on a theory of 'renewing' a revealed religion which lies at the core of its revivalism, it, once again, overlooks the fact that religions cannot be subject to 'renovations', 'restorations' or 'purifications'. Such terms are inapplicable for being contradictory to essential religion. In fact their impact is distortive.

Basically elective, neo-Islam sought various methods to justify itself, including a repetitious process of making and unmaking enemies continually to set its believers' energies free to fight, not to reconcile and compromise. It was the fault-finding method that the neo-Islamic theorists had adhered to from the beginning which made of this method an aggressive program and a bad thinking habit that would not rest until it found enemies or adversaries to confront. This was a process that was destined to continue endlessly in radicalizing and militarizing neo-Islam's zealots for an extremist march to establish a neo-Islamic state, one which is against the odds of an increasingly secularized and globalized contemporary world. Almost all neo-Islamic groups adopt militancy as a short-cut path to their ultimate goal, the creation of an Islamic state, a 'caliphate', disregarding the flaws of the historical caliphates, Arab and Turkish. Because the historical caliphates were mostly Sunni institutions, it automatically followed that working for rejuvenating one was bound to be a Sunni program, a program that combined all neo-Islamic theorists and groups by a single far-fetched purpose. For their historically bitter experience with the caliphates except for a five-year period of Ali's rule, the Shi'i Muslim revivalists do not aspire for a caliphate. Instead they have presented the model of the 'government of the Jurist'. The militarization of the neo-Islamic groups was originally inspired by the conviction of the possibility of repeating the historical Islamic conquests that had been accomplished by fierce camel-drivers under the command of the idealized Muslim caliphs. Conceived as compulsive military campaigns which were meant to reform and impose the worship of the one God, coercion was adopted by the neo-Islamists as initiator of confrontations with the 'others' who seemed to be passive and incapable of retaliation for certain weaknesses. In a word, they seemed feminine. For the conquerors, force was synonymous with masculinity, while passivity with the feminine. Neo-Islamic logic regrets and rejects the times of passivity in late Islamic history, those times which enabled the industrial West, then masculine, to impose its authority on the frail Muslim nations which were powerless in front of military coercion and masculine exploitation because they had been internally weakened. Neo-Islamists embrace the conviction that they can reverse the gender polemic and feminize the Western World, given its 'effeminate' status which is mirrored by its weaknesses and decadence. Proponents of neo-Islam attempt to utilize the frailty of Western materialistic civilization which seems to them aging and no more capable of power extension or exploitation.

If analyzed carefully with reference to its early stirrings, neo-Islam proves to be an orthodox Sunni response to its loss of state authority. Its compensatory theory was made in such a way as to restore state power to Sunni Islam after having lost it for foreign enemies due to mismanagement and corruption. From another perspective, the origins of the neo-Islamic theory hide deep in Sunni Islam's failure to maintain state power wisely, a situation which made it deserving of criticism and inviting for correction. It has always maintained a margin of self-criticism administered by the clerical elite. Once toppled, Sunni Islam resorted to innovating neo-Islam as a reformulation of itself to regain power. Neo-Islam took to protest and struggle against the foreign foes which had replaced Sunni authority, repositioning the centers of power pragmatically. Accordingly, it reversed the mechanics of opposition politics, utilizing Shi'i opposition and using its archives and expertise of political and social protest to instigate and operate neo-Islamic opposition.

As its announced program is consistent with its stated goal of establishing a global Islamic state, a caliphate, neo-Islam's outspoken aggressiveness and avowed adoption of terror planted obstacles on its own path to realize that, so far, visionary state, particularly when neo-Islam's major groups prematurely dismissed non-Sunni Muslims outside the partial and discriminatory future state of the neo-Islamic dreams.

Because neo-Islam is an imitative program, it lacks originality while its initiators can in no way be comparable to Prophet Muhammed or to his indisputably authority on the early Muslims. They prove to be dreamers who, albeit serious, do not have the vision or the genius of the real prophets. They fall short of prophethood because neo-Islam is a copy and a copy cannot be as good as the original. As mere copiers, neo-Islamic theorists differ with each other in their emphases and tactics due to the flaws of selectivity that keep on deforming their ideas and ways. This is why they went astray: while Taymiyya focused on fighting the foreign foe which had terminated the Arab monopoly of the historical Islamic state, his Wahabi successors, among other imitators focused their aggressive energies more emphatically on what appeared to them to be the imminent danger from within, that is from all the Muslims who do not abide by their black-and-white dogmatic rules. The 'struggle' changed focus consequently as the enemy of

145

Islam is no more foreign. From a Wahabi standpoint, a foreigner is no worse enemy than a Shi'i or a Sufi Muslim.

Since it is meant to renew religion by imitating a historical model to be applicable to novel circumstances, the neo-Islamic theory eventually substantiates the accusations set against it such as those of being essentially reactionary. It seeks to turn the wheel of time back to the past which is essentially an attempt to reverse progression.

Though an offshoot of neo-Islam, the Muslim Brotherhood's interpretation of the ancestral dream that which hid behind its version of neo-Islam showed a relative openness and susceptibility to the outcomes of Western democratic political traditions which deem politics a civil activity, though proposing to compensate Europe's termination of the Ottoman caliphate by another despotic caliphate, which is envisaged to be global and, naturally, no less totalitarian. The Muslim brothers are, therefore, neither Shi'i-phobic nor Sufi-phobic. The Muslim Brotherhood is, from a certain perspective, a neo-Islamic attempt to go the middle way between the *al-Qa'ida's* terrorist brand of neo-Islam and the peaceful Islam of the traditional mosque-goers. The group's millions of members aspire to realize the far-fetched dream of an Islamic world state by tolerating and merging the various and, at times, jarring sects of the Islamic world to come out with a unique 'fraternal' version of neo-Islam, one which is hoped to transcend the sectarian differences and pass the tests of domestic and global admission. The Muslim Brotherhood's neo-Islam stands undecided today, torn between its civil global aspirations, on the one hand, and the Wahabi extremism of a vast portion of its massive membership, on the other.

Only two significant patterns of behavior remain to be noted in most of the neo-Islamic terror networks: (1) The networks' ceaseless and, probably, limitless capacity to split, branch and multiply, though preserving and cherishing a unified overall medievalist vision; (2) Their appearance and growth within communities that suffer from internal divisions, especially religious or sectarian divisions.

On the one hand, dissents and splits in the terror networks arise from the neo-Islamic excessive reliance on biased and premeditated interpretations of an already hazy historical narrative, partly factual and partly the making of fiction. The so-called 'standard' histories of Islam, especially those of its early years of dissent, were inked under political pressure and state supervision by the medieval so-called 'master' historians who had collected their annals and records from an earlier species of oral historians dependent on mere memory, known as ikhbariyoun. The later written histories of the medieval master historians (al-Tabari, al-Mas'udi and al-Ya'qubi, among others) were hardly trusted by the diverse political parties and, of course, by posterity. Sources of disagreement rather than certainty, their histories could in no way serve as authentic and trustworthy bases of historical authority, though they were inadequately considered 'standard' in Islamic culture. This culture demonstrated its inability to cross the bar between antiquity and modernity by this very regressive adherence to the above dust-gathering histories. In a way, the medieval historians interposed a barrier between their confused and confusing 'tale-telling' and the crucially needed fresh light of the 'new history' of our times. Except for rare instances in the last and current centuries to critically explore and examine certain 'black holes' in the labyrinth of Islamic history made by forward-looking Muslim historians or intellectuals, no impartial or bias-free re-writing of Islamic history was attempted. Irrespective of their short comings, the medieval histories were standardized as practical experience showed that brave and objective attempts to re-read or revalue them from a scientific critical perspective were continually dismissed as suspicious, not to say heretic. Standardization led to idolization automatically; and the idol-breaking religion of Islam ended building new idols. Objective historical accounts and analyses continued to be unwelcome throughout the history of Islamic history to the present moment. But despite or, perhaps, because of this kind of standardization of the medieval historical texts, variants of interpretation followed urged by changing political interests and inconsistency, giving birth to diverse attitudes and approaches that crystallized in the fanatic and rebellious groups of later times. In a way, each group came into existence in response to a new interpretation of Islam, not as a spiritual tradition, but as history. While in the beginning of the current century, the world knew only a single terror network, al-Qa'ida, today it is busy distinguishing, grading and classifying many more networks that popped up one after the other in a row lately, producing unthought-of names such as ISIL or Khurasan.

On the other hand, we must not overlook the alarming observation that such terror networks thrive and prosper in times of turmoil and conflict within divided communities (or societies) which provide terror with the environment and stimuli it requires to exist and then to grow. Sectarianism by-produces the prerequisite aggressive atmosphere which promotes terror and rewards it, moving it steps forward from the sectarian (Sunni, Shi'i) to the broader level of the religious (Muslim, Christian), that is from the local to the regional, and then from the latter to the global. For the masses of angry young men and women in the Islamic societies, there is always the burden of a huge accumulation of grievances and social protest; and terror comes to the impoverished and hopeless youth as the one answer to their irremovable sense of futility and aimlessness.

Inadequate and regressive educational systems strengthen the urge to embrace the fanatic and the violent instead of the moderate and the calm, to be sure. No less significant is the fact that sectarian collisions are historically proven to be the bloodiest, most sadistic and the most consequential, let alone their psychological residual remnants that endure within the collective psyche throughout successive generations. Sectarianism is, unfortunately, not self-containable and self-consuming because it inevitably exports its surplus of aggressive sentiments and demonic energies outside, once any of the conflicting groups demands or aspires for help from foreign parties. Accordingly, the 'mutiny within' is translated in a new idiom that attempts to externalize its cause by seeking foreign foes to fight and, thus, to vent out its aggressive energies.

This complexity is indisputably the consequence of decades of unwise government that ignore and let go the irresponsible educational systems which produce the extremist rather than the moderate, the anarchist rather than the civil gentleman.

Appendix

Caliphess

In writing the above chapter entitled "Feminizing the West", my purpose was to demonstrate how the male-female polemic operates within the Muslim psyche with such an intensity that it outdoes almost all other 'polemics' put together. It becomes *the* decisive factor in the tense and incongruent relationships which govern the way that psyche conceives what is problematic, particularly in so far as the relationship with the Western World is concerned, and that world's ignorance of Islam's roots which strike deep in 'Arabia Deserta' where gender and sex were eternal certainties as immovable as those of life and death which left a durable impact on the Muslim mind and its worldview. As a faith, Islam is the fruition of the dry desert in almost everyone of its tenets, from the imagery of its holy book to its history, carrying the legacy of that cruel environment and its patient and swift people who were called by European sources after their legacy as the wandering 'sons of Ishmael' or the 'Saracens'.

A knowledgeable scholar of the histories of the Middle East would never find it rational to speak of a 'caliphess', in analogy with king/queen and lion/lioness. Such a feminine derivation from the term 'caliph' can in no way be permissible or even comprehensible to the Muslim mind due to the ancient biases of the desert nomadic existence of the Arabs. The Arabic term, *khalifeh* (meaning, caliph), though in the feminine form, is applicable only to the male heads of the historical Islamic state which Muhammed's companions founded after his death. In the Islamic lore, there is no sign whatsoever that would suggest the possibility of a woman ruler. The authority and, indeed, leaderships at large are the monopoly of men only, a situation that crystallizes in the smallest social unit, the family, and it spirals upward to the afore-mentioned prerequisite conditions for nominating a caliph, those conditions which make no mention of the probability of replacing the word 'man' by 'individual' or 'person' to make it attainable for the 'system' to transcend its gender prejudices in leadership and power administration.

Such an age-old tradition was continually supported by proverbial sayings which deem it a bad omen for a community to be ruled by a woman, a residual remnant of the Bedouin father-headed family system of old. No less significant should, of course, be the prevalent undemocratic form of family organization that survived all social transitions to continue to the present moment unabated in the Islamic societies. The paternal family system existed before the advent of Islam in Arabia, not simply as a desert phenomenon, but also as a shared legacy of the Judaeo-Christian religious tradition which also had its desert coloration to be sure. It was, therefore, the common family model throughout the 'Bible lands', Islamic, Jewish or Christian. More significant might be the fact that the paternal family model projected itself in the dominant paternal Middle-Eastern societies today where the monarch or president continually emphasizes a self-image of a father figure who would purposefully address his subjects as 'my children' (*abna'i*), a self-made fatherhood, blessed by both the nomadic and the religious traditions.

Before Islam the Arabs had maintained a grim, essentially nomadic, objectification of women which amounted to the loathsome practice of burying some of the newly born female infants alive (*wa'd al-banat*).[1] Histories state that women, like goods or riches, had a marketable and tradable value. In those ancient times, they were given as reparation to settle tribal disputes or to pay off one's creditors.[2] Such abuses are still practiced in the tribal communities of vast portions of the Middle East, and is known in Iraq as compensation (*faşl*), which means making good the loss of another clan by compensating it by a young woman.

The survival of such backward traditions means that the problem of bias against women is not merely historical only because it surfaces in contemporary life as well. Note the irony of having an Islamic country (Pakistan) that was ruled for years by a strong educated woman, Benazir Bhutto, whose popularity and legacy had outshone those of the male politicians put together, but was not good enough for the neo-Islamist groups who killed her and moved on to ban education for the young Muslim girls, as was the case when a school bus crammed with school girls, was attacked by a gunman who was destined to be the head of the Pakistan Taliban later. He wounded a young girl, Malala, and, to his disappointment, she survived and her case was utilized by the Western and world media so as to make her a hero considerable for the Peace Nobel Prize. In symbolic terms, the distance that extends between Malala and Bhutto is very much reflective of the improvements Islam had introduced to the status of women and the reactionary debasement of women which neo-Islam tried hard to impose on Muslim societies for several purposes, including the one we have discussed in chapter V.

In this context, it should be significant to find out if the above neo-Islamic low opinion of women was an original Middle-Eastern social flaw, and whether it was inclusive of all the cultures of the region. History could provide us with meaningful clues concerning this controversial subject. It could show us clearly whether the laws of Islam (the *shari'a*) concerning women were extensions and reinforcements of former Bedouin traditions or reactions against them. To review some significant comparisons between pre-Islam and post-Islam societies is feasible for this matter. In comparison to the malpractices of the earlier epoch, the Islamic tradition proves to be way better.[3] The 'selective' method of comparison that follows should in no way obscure the fact that the improvements Islam introduced on the status of women were relative because in ancient Middle-Eastern civilizations women entertained such a high status that they transcended the earthly to the heavenly, thanks to the recurrent female symbolism of fertility, becoming goddesses or goddess-like soothsayers as was the case with the Sumerian goddess *Inanna*, the predecessor of the well-known Akkadian, Assyrian and Babylonian omnipotent goddesses of fertility, love, war and sex.[4] Ishtar's grasp over the interrelated powers of sex, love and fertility was by no means insignificant in this context because in ancient Babylonian lore there were goddesses who resided, like Lord Tennyson's the 'Lady of shallot', half-way between earth and heaven, on top of the ziggurats and, there they occasionally copulated with handsome earthly men who had to climb the exhaustive stairs to reach them for the physical reward. Such lustful demigoddesses served as go-betweens linking the ancient Mesopotamian two spheres of existence, a function which entailed no loss of female physical desires or sacrifice of the mating ecstasies. Such women were both celestial and human.

If women could be of such transcendental nature in the ancient river-valley cultures, then why should they not be queens or empresses? This was the case in the fertile portions of the region long before the advent of Islam in a small forgotten corner of the Sahara of Arabia. No survey of Mesopotamian legacies would ever fail to recall Samiramis, the Babylonian queen who ruled supreme in the year 600 B.C. No less significant was the queen of Sheeba, *Balqīs*, who was born in Mareb (in today's Yemen), and ruled supreme to extend her reign transcontinentally from Arabia Felix to Ethiopia in the tenth century B.C. To retreat to ancient Egypt, one would be surprised by the numerous female pharaohs, including the unforgettable names of those who are still remembered in modern popular culture like Cleopatra, Nefertiti and Hatshepsut. The above brief survey would make it obvious that the diversity of perception between the people of the desert and those of the irrigated valleys, owed much of its nature to environmental differences. In the fertile valleys women (symbolic of fertility) were highly valued, while in the wastelands of the vast deserts they were looked down at and badly treated as burdens, not life-givers.

The advent of Islam, the religion which later became

the dominant faith in most of the Middle East, served not only as a demarcation line between past and present in so far as the desert culture was concerned, but, being the child of the desert, it pursued and generalized several of the desert values on nations that had nothing to do with desert nomadic existence formerly, This was an aspect of the double impact it had handled and kept on expanding on nations of different cultures. For an instance, Islam's permission of polygamy, though conditioned, is a desert legacy because it had been widely and limitlessly practiced before. It was on this basis that Prophet Muhammed married several times, stating that "I am but a human being like you". Notable for the purpose of this discussion is the number of the wives he was said to have taken to the wedlock. Most historians believe that they were ten wives, probably for he had an inheritance crisis because only his first wife carried children, except for the Coptic Maria who gave birth to a male baby who died two years later. This crisis proved to be politically consequential as Muhammed's only remaining child was a female, Fatima. She got married to his cousin, Ali, whose two sons (Hasan and Husayn) were eventually Muhammed's only male successors. They were, therefore, championed by the Shi'i Muslims as his only legitimate heirs for their being a resumption of the prophet's line via his only daughter.

Prophet Muhammed's other marriages had ignited much controversy then as they did later. Though religionists justified several of his marriages on a political basis to distance him from the accusations of sensuality, his domestic enemies and the Western Orientalists later brought up those accusations to devalue his character. The religionists respond to the accusations by stating that he had no intercourse with most of his wives because he married them for political purposes: to pacify a certain group or to win another to his side during the hard times of spreading the faith. To verify their hypothesis, they recurrently recall his marriage to a Jewess, Safiyya, and to the above-mentioned Coptic Christian, Maria. It should also be of significance to refer to his marriages to the daughters of two of the most influential of his chieftains, Aysha and Hafsa. The former was his first successor's daughter, while the latter was his second successor's daughter.

Aysha was of special significance for the political role she played after the death of her prophetic husband who had married her while she was still very young, allegedly about nine years old only. She was noted for her beauty and youthful vigor, traits that hid behind accusing her of adultery, being married to an old man. This accusation was based on the so-called *ifk* incident. It so happened that she and her young camel-driver were separated from the desert caravan which had included them and lost track of the rest of the travelers for a night. Rumors irrevocably followed and made public to the community which began suspecting the incident till a *Qurā'nic* verse was inspired to the prophet, stating for a fact that all of his wives had been divinely wed and, therefore, were the chaste 'mothers of all the faithful'. They transcended all types of misconduct and unfaithfulness by a divine revelation which no one could doubt, of course. Known for her fair complexion as (*al-humayra'*), Aysha assumed a an active political role after Muhammed's death when she incited a number of her husband's former companions and mobilized them to rebel against Ali's assumption of power, allegedly because he had suggested to the prophet that he might better divorce her on the basis of the above-narrated incident.

The desert notion concerning the vulnerability of women to sensuous seduction is demonstrated clearly in the above incident which was exploited politically in the succeeding ages of Islamic history. It might be of some significance for an understanding of the major division between Sunni and Shi'i Muslims to recall the above *ifk* incident and its backfire as a polarizing political element in later times.

Another important cause behind the schism, which involved manipulating women, was the unforgettable martyrdom of Ali's son, al-Husayn, on rebelling against the second Umayyad caliph who had been appointed on a hereditary basis by his father, introducing the hereditary royal system to the caliphate for the first time in Islamic history. It was after crushing al-Husayn's rebellion, that his female companions (sisters, daughters and wife) were taken captives from the bloody battle site at Karbala to the capital in Syria as trophies of victory, following in the footsteps of targeting the powerless women by the victors that had long been established in the history of the Middle East. This was another offshoot of the desert legacy because it was considered the greatest of insults for a community to capture its women folk by a foe. Husayn's women were taken to the newly enthroned caliph at Damascus, Yezeed. This Yezeed was anxiously waiting for the news of killing his major rival and of humiliating him and his supporters by taking his women into captivity. Yezeed was reported to have been the personification of libertine behavior for his excessive pursuit of women, wine and poetic entertainments, the three most forbidden fruits of orthodox Islam. Though becoming the head of the

Islamic state, Yazeed was said to have drunk heavily and indulged in forbidden pre-Islamic knightly pleasures and lavish soirees. Conceived by the faithful as reviving the bad habits of pre-Islamic times, he served a vulnerable target for all kinds of attacks and criticism. To further distort his image, some of his critics claimed that he had been in love with his own maternal aunt and that he improvised sensuous love poems for her. But, one should acknowledge the fact that, despite all of his disgraceful indulgences, Yezeed tried hard to resolve the age-old animosity between his and his rival's family (Umayyads vs. Hashemites) by the bond of marriage when he proposed marriage to his martyred rival's sister, the brave Zayneb. Her harsh denial of his proposal intensified the everlasting quarrel between David and Saul, and, of course, between Sunnis and Shi'is by extension. Considering its circumstances, this was a very immoral and senseless incident; yet, had she yielded to his advances, this saintly woman would have changed the course of Islamic history, once and forever, by giving birth to future caliphs who were the fruition of a marriage union between the two cousins, though opposing families.

Caliph Yazeed had served as an outrageous precedent for a number of irreligious caliphs who followed him. Irreligious behavior in the history of the caliphate as an institution implied weakness of leadership. Yezeed and his likes were irresponsible libertines who were fond of luxurious good times, leaving the serious matters of the state to their chieftains and aides. Both of the Arab hereditary caliphates, Umayyad and Abbasid, had begun impressively strong, and then they succumbed to the insistent factors of decadence which went up and down in proportion with the power of the person of the caliph. The last Umayyad caliph who, ironically, inherited the name of his great grandfather, the founder of the dynasty's rule, Mu'awiyya, was so weak in the eyes of his contemporaries that they gave him the nickname of 'the donkey'.

Like a stream which begins its flow strongly, it ends up weak. The state-building founders establish their dynasty rules vigorously, and then they are followed by weak successors who waste their predecessors' achievements rapidly. This recurrent historical pattern applies to the Abbasid dynasty that replaced the Umayyad, While the founders had built a global empire, their late caliphs indulged in the lavish entertainments of female singers (*qiyān*) and belly-dancers, among other entertainers who used to be sent to them from the remote parts of the vast empire by governors and dignitaries as gifts and emblems of allegiance.

Despite the problems concerning the authorship and authenticity of *The Thousand Nights and a Night*, better known in European languages as *The Arabian Nights*, this gem of folk literature mirrored the widespread social laxity and sensuality which had overwhelmed the late Abbasid state and paved the way for the foreign foe, the Mongols, to storm the capital, Baghdad, and put an end to the empire in 1258. Decadence accompanied the parallel deterioration of the status of women as they were conceived in lewd and physical terms mostly. As mirrored in *The Nights* and other folkloric works like the *maqamat*, women were once again objectified and dehumanized to the extent of being turned marketable and exchangeable. This profligate conception was only halfway to the deterioration that followed during the Ottoman era when the 'seraglio' became no more synonymous with the Turkish caliph's domestic accessories, but also with his province-rulers' (viceroys or *walis*) and with those of the rich and the powerful elite, each one of them having his *harem* portion at home, full with silk furnishing, Turkish baths and, above all, the eunuchs who were ever dedicated to cater to the master's desires. The surgeon specialized in sterilizing the blond young men abducted very young from remote regions like Georgia or Chechnya to serve the caliph's women, was known as the *kheswenji* and he used to be an indispensible member of the Ottoman court for his invaluable services of providing the sultan's female family members (*sultanas*) with sterile handsome male servants. This prolonged phase of caliphate deterioration witnessed as well the rejuvenation of slavery in an unprecedented tempo. The *Kheswenjis* were the Muslim equivalents of medieval Christian Europe's chastity belts. Which are still on display in museums.

Female slaves also brought from as far as Africa, Caucasia and other remote regions, being status symbols, complemented the panorama of tormented beauties and forsaken womanhood in those times. This tradition is allegedly still followed by the rich in a number of Islamic societies to the present day.

The concept of honor commonly held among the Middle-Eastern nations is mainly inherited from the pre-Islamic desert legacies that were reinforced by Islam's sanctification of the paternal family model as the basic social unit. This implies that the family is conceived as the sanctified container of its members' purity of genus. Any sexual intercourse which is made outside this carefully guarded container, particularly when it results in the mixing of bloods of strangers, by adultery for instance, is deemed as an irremovable ignominy. Though ascribed to the religious traditions common in the region, this concept of lineal purity may help us trace the worst of the Middle-Eastern nations' fears, that of war captivity by an enemy of a different racial or tribal origin because this is the severest humiliation that a nation or a tribe might suffer, particularly when the captives were women, (*alsabi*).One should note the burdensome captivities which are still painfully recalled by the peoples of the region. When a woman is raped by an enemy or a stranger, she would be seen to have lost her purity, and to have been tainted together with the lineal purity of the family. Prostitution was and is practiced in the Middle East; and copulations with prostitutes are generally not condemned or despised, probably, because prostitutes were seen as common or public 'property' whose 'profession' does not cause shame to anyone, particularly when prostitutes begin their profession after being disowned by their families to distance them from familial sanctuary. It is, therefore, the greatest shame a family would suffer when it is looked down at for suspicions hovering round the 'light virtue' of a sister, a mother, a daughter or a wife. If the family male members are unable to protect their women, they would have to suffer the misfortune of being considered cowards or unmanly; that is, not worthy of trust or respect. A male's fear of being disrespected for the uncommitted behavior of a sister or a daughter could lead to some of the bloodiest and most tragic of crimes, those which are known in the Middle East as 'honor murders' or more literally, the 'shame laundering crimes'. Such killings executed by the brother on his sister, for instance, are dealt with in the courts of law mildly as 'understandable' codes of the tribal traditions of the 'conservative' society. One may find an 'honor murderer' bragging among others for his ability to 'white wash' the shame away from the family reputation. Honor went through various conceptual changes and modifications in history, fluctuating in ups and downs with the conflict between the desert nomadic culture, on the one hand, and the cultures of the settled nations of the fertile river valleys, on the other. As the desert culture proved to be stronger than the settled one, the concept of honor settled down among the region's societies limited within the scope of sexual behavior eventually, thanks to the major religious systems which had been themselves inspired by the desert or semi-desert environment. Women always have to handle the burden of 'honor', because it relies mainly on the observation of their 'chastity'. Adultery fire-fixes an irremovable 'scarlet letter' on a woman's bosom, to recall Nathaniel Hawthorne's classic.

Within such a social milieu, the outcome of the age-old mixed-up concepts of the sex-based honor, women became the ultimate victims not only because they are supposedly entrusted with the dark man's honor, but also because they are sought by 'outsiders' as the softest targets in, say, a family's makeup, a target that can be or breached by the rival community, group or enemy to practice authority on that weakened family.

Although arranged marriages are customarily adopted

by the ruling and powerful families, the way Muhammed had used them for political or economic purposes, they have become a common practice today among the 'royal' families which were enthroned by the last century's super powers in the aftermath of the First World War The royals' pursuance of such marriages are usually motivated by the above-mentioned keenness on keeping an impenetrable strong blood-bond which is supposed to make them unbreakable marriages, particularly when followed and enhanced by children. Kinships which grow out of such marriages are another form of power in the Islamic and Middle-Eastern countries, reminders of the tribal kinship of pre-Islam Arabia. In societies that are virtually unable to break free from the resilient tribal values and behavioral codes of conduct, blood relationships and similar primordial bonds rely heavily on women. Women are always seen as double-edged weapons for such bond-building purposes and for their vulnerability in such backward societies.

Women's misconceived 'vulnerability' to persuasions

is used by political enemies each against the other, a phenomenon which is embodied in the 'operations' of the governmental secret services. Not only are women targeted as soft spots, they are also directed to target the rival by such agencies. This may shed light on the frequent honor crimes committed by politicians or army officers to terminate the source of possible disgrace. The abuse of women by such security apparatuses proved to be penetrative and effective in conservative societies that equate sex with honor. To direct a young and handsome security officer to seduce a woman belonging to a rival or a potential enemy became a common practice to obtain information or to threaten the enemy by filming her in the sexual act and use the film to blackmail the foe. Stories of army officers or opposition leaders finding such films of their daughters, wives or sisters 'in the act' on their doorsteps or in their mailboxes became common in the dispiriting narrative of the political rivalries of the region's countries. Public disgrace is one of the terrifying tools that could be used against a political rival; and women are especially targeted and utilized to work out such threats.

Although conceived as vulnerable soft spots in political rivalries, women also enjoy their families' care, not for their personal value, but rather for their reproductive and genital roles in the preservation of the familial or clan nexus, in addition to the afore-mentioned use for alliances of powerful families through marriages. This consideration may shed light on the utmost care such families take to guard their womenfolk from outsiders, lest they should be seduced into illicit relationships of potential harm to their families' reputation. The protective alertness of men may amount to compulsively isolate their womenfolk from the society at large, a situation which sheds light on the emphasis such families lay on the isolated schooling of their girls, a private kind of schooling that must be administered by women only, from the primary stages to the graduate and postgraduate ones, an updated reproduction of the *harem*. This is the reason that the daughters of such powerful families develop a kind of psychological retardation which stems from isolation and from the consequent the illusion of being descendants of a different species of men, 'superior' to others.

When appointed chairman of the English Department, College of Education for Women (Baghdad University), the present author was surprised by discovering that he had to run two English Departments, one for the commoners' daughters, and another for the ruling Tikriti elites' daughters. The first is the 'public' department, while the second is the double department; and girls belonging to the latter do not mix with their equals in the former at all to preserve their immunity. They have their own classes and premises. The double-department situation began years before the above unfortunate appointment. It started when Saddam's daughter (Raghad) had completed her high school and wished to study English in the university. As the daughter of and idolized leader, this poor Raghad was also idolized because all the daughters, sisters and wives of the Tikriti circle, who wished to go to the university, followed into her footsteps till the 'minority of one' carried in its high tide tens of the girls of Saddam's ministers, bodyguards, cousins and aides who made a whole 'shadow' department of English, fully equipped with female-teachers and administers. Even the drivers who brought the students to the shadow department had to be women.

The above surprise, when contemplated deeply later in time, showed the survival of the above-mentioned seraglio mentality of the Ottoman *harem.* The isolationist tradition continued unabated because those who are in power in the Middle East are continually haunted by the specter of their womenfolk being lured into flirtatious affairs which could harm the ruler's honor, a possibility that continued to be scary to rulers from the time Iraq's King Faisal I.'s daughter eloped with a Greek waiter from the hotel she was sent to for a vacation.

Originally derived from a nomadic desert tradition which the ruling families hold dear and impose on their subjects, the idea of womanhood in the Middle East and the Islamic World in general remain captive to backwardness and reaction as long as the ruling groups continue resisting new values, using the huge oil revenues to preserve and cherish an ancestral medieval dream that can neither be realized nor imitated in replica. The rulers' imprisonment of his womenfolk automatically gives him and his men a sense of freedom, resting assured that his women are tightly guarded and protected. This freedom, however, stems from the feeling that he is now set free to enjoy his own adventures with the women of his powerless subjects. Note the 'Don Juan' phenomenon which is currently common among several of the leaders and their sons, brothers or relatives, particularly in the Middle East. It may account for the amorous adventures of some of them personally, and for the polygamy of others. Against this kind of self-given freedom with the women of their subjects, the royal or stately womenfolk are kept hidden and, literally, 'invisible'. Some such 'Muslim' royals or statesmen are said to keep numerous wives in addition to the female slaves who are literally 'bought' for them for passing momentary desires. The outcome of such lustful pursuits would, of course, be regiments of children, whose high numbers would turn into a burden on the nation, considering the privileges they entertain on the account of the commoners. Sons, brothers, cousins and other relatives of the despot are usually trusted with the important offices of the government, civil and military. No less significant are the young 'Don Juans', the offshoots of totalitarian dictatorships, who also wish to follow in the footsteps of their elders or even excel them, if possible.

Saddam Hussein had a secret *affaire d' amour* which he uncovered in a novelette published under a penname, *katebuha*. His sons Uday and Qusay were known for their libertine adventures which involved using social clubs and sports to hunt the prettiest young women to the extent that seriously conservative and respectable families abstained from attending such public places or activities for fear that their daughters might be pinpointed by the President's sons' poisonous gaze.

No survey of the history of authority and power in the Middle East would ever fail to demonstrate the consistent decline of the status of women from ancient to current times via the era of the advent of Islam which followed in the footsteps of the monotheistic religious traditions in their adoption of the paternal family model as the basic social unit. This gave rise to the common concepts of honor, shame and morality, those which objectified and victimized women in accordance with a simplistic polemics of masculine aggressive power vs. feminine passive fragility. Throughout Middle-Eastern history, the performers were mostly men, while the receivers of the performances were women, unless both performed off-stage and their actions were only reported. The goddesses of ancient Babylonia who had prostituted themselves with earthly men were eventually brought down to earth by religious and social traditions that substituted the heavenly 'Blessed Damozels'[5] by the woman behind the veil.

End Notes

Notes to Chapter I.

(After the Prophet)

1. Quoted in Muhammed A. Al Da'mi, *Arabian Mirrors and Western Soothsayers: Nineteenth-Century Literary Approaches to Arab-Islamic History* (NY: Peter Lang Publishing, 2002), p. 7.

2. Quoted in *ibid.,* p. 54.

3. *Ibid.,* 54.

4. Ralph Waldo Emerson, *The Complete Works of Ralph Waldo Emerson*, vol. X (Boston: Houghton, Mifflin and Company, 1904), p. 177.

5. For an idea on this seasonal caravan trade, consult: Muhammed Al Da'mi, *The Other Islam: Shi'ism: From Idol-Breaking to Apocalyptic Mahdism.* Revised

Edition (Bloomington, IN.: Authorhouse, 2013), pp. 51-3.

6. For an analysis of Carlyle's theory of the Hero, consult: B.H. Lehman, *Carlyle's Theory of the Hero* (Durham; NC.: Duke Univ. Press, 1928).

7. Quoted in: www.muslm.org/bb/archives/index.php/t-315980.html. (Sep. 28, 2013).

8. Thomas Carlyle, *On Heroes, Hero-Worship and the Heroic in History* (London: Collins' Clear-Type Press, ND), pp. 90-1.

9. John Henry Newman, *Historical Sketches*, vol. I (Westminster: Christian Classics, 1970), pp. 175-6.

10. Quoted in William F. Tucker, *Mahdis and Millenarians: Shi'ite Extremists in Early Muslim Iraq* (Cambridge: Cambridge Univ. Press, 2008), p. 134.

Notes to Chapter II

(Secret Societies)

1. For an idea on the lengthy era of civil unrest and popular upheavals, consult: Muhammed Al Da'mi, *The Other Islam: Shi'ism: From Idol-Breaking to Apocalyptic Mahdism*. Revised edition (Bloomington, IN.: Authorhouse, 2013), chapter III, in particular.

2. Washington Irving, *Mahomet and His Successors*, vol. II (NY: The Continental Press, ND), pp. 463-4.

3. John Henry Newman, *Historical Sketches*, vol. I (Westminster, MD.: Christian Classics, 1970), pp. 175-6.

4. Consult: wikipedia.org8wiki/Brethren-of-Purity. (Sep. 1, 2013).

5. *Ibid.*

6. Quoted in *ibid.*

7. Quoted in Roger Allen, *An Introduction to Arabic*

Literature (Cambridge: Cambridge Univ. Press, 2005), p. 41.

8. wikipedia.org8wiki/Brethren-of-Purity. (Sep. 1, 2013).

9. *Ibid.*

10. *Ibid.*

11. Quoted in *ibid.*

12. *Ibid.*

13. Bernard Lewis, *The Crisis of Islam: Holy war and Unholy Terror* (NY: Random House Trade Paperbacks, 2003), p. 144.

14. Jefferson Gray, "Holy Terror: The Rise of the Order of Assassins", *Al-Mashriq*, vol. 10, no. 40 (March, 2012), p. 67.

15. *Ibid.*, p. 73.

16. See *ibid.*, p. 74.

17. Lewis, pp. 144-6.

Notes to Chapter III

(The Growth of Neo-Islam)

1. Consult: Gorge A. Barton, *Religions of the World* (Chicago: Chicago University Press, 1993); Karen Armstrong, *A History of God* (NY: Alfred A. Knopf, 1993), pp. 132-169, and Huston Smith, *The World's Religions: Our Great Traditions* (NY: Harper Collins Publishers, 1991).

2. Consult: Muhammed Al Da'mi, *The Other Islam; Shi'ism: From Idol-Breaking to Apocalyptic Mahdism.* Revised edition (Bloomington, IN: Authorhouse, 2013), pp. 77-80.

3. *Ibid.,* pp. 140-2.

4. Consult: en.wikipedia.org/wiki/Ibn-Taymiyyah. (July 13, 2013).

5. *Ibid.*

6. *Ibid.*

7. See: Al Da'mi, pp. 109-128.

8.	Consult: on Wikipedia.org/wiki/Muslim-Brotherhood. (July 12, 2013).

9.	Muhammed Al Da'mi, *Caught in a Dream: Nine Paradoxes from Middle-Eastern Medievalism* (Bloomington, IN.: Authorhouse, 2013), pp. 2-3.

10.	William L. Cleveland, *A History of the Middle East* (Boulder, CO: Westview, 2004), pp. 14-15.

11.	Natana J. Delong-Bas, *Wahhabi Islam: From Revival to Global Jihad* (Oxford: OUP, 2004), pp. 82-91.

12.	Hamid Algar, *Wahhabism: A Critical Essay* (NY: Oneonta, 2001), p. 20.

13.	*Ibid.,* p.22.

14.	*Ibid.,* p. 10.

15.	De Long-bas, pp. 4, 51-3 and 248-9.

16.	Algar, pp. 19-23.

17.	*Ibid.,* p. 19.

18.	De Long-bas, pp. 197-200 and 215.

19.	Algar, pp. 20-1.

20. See: en.wikipedia.org/wiki/committee_for_the_ promotion_of_Virtue-and_the_ Prevention _of_Vice. (Sept. 5, 2013)

Note to Chapter IV
(Muslim Brotherhood)

1. on.wikipedia.org/wiki/Muslim_Brotherhood. (July 12, 2013).

2. *Ibid.*

3. *Ibid.*

4. *Ibid.*

5. *Ibid.*

6. Bernard Lewis, *The Crisis of Islam: Holy War and Unholy Terror* (NY: Random House Trade Paperbacks, 2003), p. 78.

7. *Ibid.*

8. The author met a number of young men in Suva, Fiji

(1981), who presented themselves as members of the Muslim Brotherhood.

9. Quoted in: http://www.economist.com/node/21547853. Nov. 13, 2013.

10. *Ibid.*

11. Andrew C. McCarthy, *The Grand Jihad: How Islam and the Left Sabotage America* (NY: Encounter Books, 2010), pp. 83-4 and 303-5. This book gives the impression of being written for a wholesale critique of the Muslim Brotherhood.

12. http://www.economist.com/node/21547853, Nov. 13, 2013.

13. en.wikipedia.org/wiki/Muslim_Brotherhood. July 7, 2013.

14. http://www.businessweek.com/articles/2012-04-19/ the economicvision-of-egypt-muslim-brotherhood-millionaires. Nov. 3, 2013.

Notes to Chapter V

(Feminizing the West)

1. The tribes of al-Aws and al-Khazraj.

2. Consult: Roger Allen, *An Introduction to Arabic Literature* (Cambridge: The University Press, 2005), pp. 17 and 72.

3. For a discussion of this theme, see: Muhammed Al Da'mi, *The Other Islam; Shi'ism: From Idol-Breaking to Apocalyptic Mahdism*. Revised edition (Bloomington, IN.: Authorhouse, 2013), pp 149-150.

4. Consult: Muhammed Al Da'mi, "The Harem in the Colonizer's Eye", *The Middle East Quarterly,* 3, no. 11 (1996), pp. 32-40.

5. Quoted in Muhammed Al Da'mi, *Arabian Mirrors and the Western Soothsayers: Nineteenth-Century Literary Approaches to Arab-Islamic History* (NY: Peter Lang, 2002),

Notes to the Appendix (Caliphess)

1. Muhammed Al Da'mi, *The Other Islam; Shi'ism: From Idol-Breaking to Apocalyptic Mahdism.* Revised Edition (Bloomington, IN: Authorhouse, 2013), p.70.

2. William L. Cleveland, *A History of the Modern Middle East*, 3rd edition (Boulder, CO: Westview, 2004), pp. 30.

3. See: *Ibid.,* pp. 29-30; and Al Da'mi, pp. 66-7.

4. Consult: en.wikipedia.org/wiki/Ishtar. Retrieved on July 14, 2013.

5. This is the title of one of the poems of D. G. Rossetti, a late Victorian poet.

Guide to Further Readings

Abrahamian, Ervand. *Khomeinism: Essays on the Islamic Republic*. Berkeley: University of California Press, 1993.

Acar, Ismail. "Interactions between Prophet Muhammed and Christians, *Al-Mashriq*. Vol 10, no 38 (Sep. 2011), 85-90.

Ajami, Leila. *Women and Gender in Islam*. New Heaven: Yale University Press. 1992.

Al Da'mi, Muhammed. "Morris' Idea of the East and His Anti-Colonial Attitudes", *Abhath Al-Yarmouk,* 4. No. 2 (1986), 47-58.

_____. "The Harem in the Colonizer's Eye", *The Middle East Quarterly*. 3, no. 11 (1996). 32-40.

_____. *Arabian Mirrors and Western Soothsayers: Nineteenth-Century Literary Approach to Arab-Islamic History*. N.Y.: Peter Lang, 2002.

_____. "The Aryan Dimension of Arnold's Interest

in the Arab-Islamic East", *Al-Mashriq*, vol. I., no, 2 (Sept., 2002), 24-30.

_____. *Caught in a Dream: None Paradoxes from Middle-Eastern Medievalism*. Bloomington IN.: Authorhouse, 2013.

_____. *The Other Islam; Shi'ism: From Idol-Breaking to Apocalyptic Mahdism*. Revised edition. Bloomington, IN.: Authorhouse, 2013.

_____. *The Other Spiritualities of the Middle East: The Minority Religious Traditions of the Ahl-e Haqq, the Mandaens and the Yezidis*. Denver, CO: Outskirts, 2013.

Algar, Hamid. *Wahhabism: A Critical Essay*. N. Y.: Oneonta, 2002.

Allen, Roger. *An Introduction to Arabic Literature*. Cambridge: Cambridge University Press, 2000.

Allison, Graham. *Nuclear Terrorism: The Ultimate Preventable Catastrophe*. NY: Times Books, 2004.

Arjomand, Said Amir. *The Shadow of God and the Hidden Imam*. Chicago: Univ. of Chicago Press, 1984.

Armstrong, Karen. *A History of God*. NY: Alfred A. Knopf, 1993.

Aslan Reza. *No God but God: The Origin, Evolution, and Future of Islam*. New York: Random House, 2006.

Atwan, Abdel Bari. *The Secret History of al-Qaeda*. Berkeley: University of California Press, 2006.

Bablawi, Hazem, and Luciani, Giacomo, eds. *The Rentier State*. London: Croom Helm, 1987.

Baker, James A., and Lee H. Hamilton, Co-Chairs, *The Iraq Study Group Report: The Way Forward—A New Approach*. NY: Vintage Books, 2006.

Barton, George A. *The Religions of the World*. Chicago: Univ. of Chicago Press, 1929.

Beinin, Joel, and Strok, Joe. *Political Islam: Essays from Middle East Report*.

Berkeley: University of California Press, 1997.

Bell, Gertrude. *Great Britain and Iraq: An Experiment*

in Anglo-Asiatic Relations. London: Round Table, published anonymously, 1924.

_____. *The Desert and the Sown.* NY: Cooper Square Press, 2001.

Benjamin, Daniel, and Steven Simon. *The Age of Sacred Terror.* N.Y.: Random House, 2002.

_____. *The Next Attack: The Failure of the War on Terror and a Strategy for Getting It Right.* NY: Times Books, 2005.

Bergen, Peter L. *Holy War, Inc: Inside the Secret World of Osama Bin Laden.* N.Y. Free press, 2001.

Berlinski, Claire. *Menace in Europe: Why the Continent's Crisis Is America's Too.* NY: Crown Forum Books. 2007.

Bernsten, Gary, and Ralph Pezzulo. *Jawbreaker: The Attack on Bin Laden and al-Qaeda:A Personal Account by CIA's Key Field Commander.* NY: Three Rivers Press, 2006.

Bevis, Richard. "Spiritual Geography: C.M. Doughty and the Land of the Arabs", *Victorian Studies,* 16 (Dec. 1972), 163-181.

Blankley, Tony. *The West's Last Chance: Will We Win the Clash of Civilizations?* Washington, D.C.: Regnery Publications, 2005.

Bodkin, Maud. *Archetypal Patterns in Poetry: Psychological Studies of Imagination.* London: OUP, 1965.

Brockelmann, Carl. *History of the Islamic Peoples.* Trans. Carmichael & M. Perlmann, London: Routledge & Kegan Paul, 1980.

Brynen, Rex, et al., eds. *Political Liberalization and Democratization in the Arab World.* Vol. 1: *Theoretical Perspectives.* Boulder, Colo.: Lynne Rienner, 1995.

Burton, Richard. "Terminal Essay", in *The Book of the Thousand Nights and a Night, v*ol. 8. London: H. S. Nicholas Ltd., 1897, 59-230.

Cambridge History of Islam. 4 vols. London: Cambridge Univ. Press, 1970.

Carlyle, Thomas. *On Heroes, Hero-Worship, and the Heroic in History.* London: Collins' Clear-Type Press, N.D.

Clarke, Richard A. *Against All Enemies: Inside America's War on Terror.* N.Y.: Free Press. 2004.

Cleveland, William *L.A. History of the Modern Middle East.* 3rd ed. Boulder, CO.: Westview, 2004.

Coll, Steve. *Ghost Wars: The Secret History of the CIA: Afghanistan and Bin Laden, from the Soviet Invasion to September 10, 2001.* NY: Penguin, 2004.

Crone, Patricia, and Martin Hinds, *God's Caliph: Religious Authority in the First Centuries of Islam.* Cambridge: Cambridge University Press, 1986.

Daniel, Norman. *Islam and the West: The Making of an Image. Edinburgh.* Edinburgh Univ. Press, 1960.

De Long-Bas, Natana J. *Wahhabi Islam: From Revival to Global Jihad.* Oxford: OUP, 2004.

Dray, William. *Perspectives on History.* London: Routledge & Kegan Paul, 1980.

Dulop, D. M. "Some Remarks on Weil's History of the Caliphs", *Historians of the Middle East.* Bernard Lewis and P.M. Holt, eds. London: OUP, 1962, 315-329.

Elshtain, Jean Bethke. *Just War Against Terror: The Burden of American Power in a Violent World.* NY: Basic Books, 2003.

Emerson, Ralph Waldo. *The Complete Works of Ralph Waldo Emerson.* Boston: Houghton, Mifflin and Company, 1904.

Faris, N. A. "Development in Arab Historiography as Reflected in the Struggle Between Ali and Mu'awiya", *Historians of the Middle East.* London: OUP, 1962, 435-441.

Fromkin, David. *A Peace to End All Peace: Creating the Modern Middle East.* N.Y.: Henry Holt and Co., 1989.

Gerges, Fawwaz. *The Far Enemy: Why Jihad Went Global.* N.Y.: Cambridge University Press, 2005.

Gibb, H.A.R. *Islam: A Historical Survey.* Oxford: UOP, 1949.

Goldberg, Ellis, et al. *Rules and Rights in the Middle East: Democracy, Law, and Society.* Seattle: University of Washington Press, 1993.

Gordon, Joel. *Nasser's Blessed Movement: Egypt's Free Officers and the July Revolution.* NY: OUP, 1992.

Gramm, Kent. *Gettysburg: A Meditation on War and Values.* Bloomington: Indiana University Press, 1994.

Gray, Jefferson. "Holy Terror: The Rise of the Order of Assassins", *Al-Mashriq.* Vol. 10. No. 40 (March, 2012), 67-78.

Grunebaum, G.E. Von. "Self-Image and Approach to History", *Historians of The Middle East.* London: OUP, 1962, 457-483.

Habeck, Mary. *Knowing the Enemy: Jihadist Ideology and the War on Terror.* New Haven, Conn.: Yale University Press, 2006.

Halliday, Fred. *Islam and the Myth of Confrontation: Religion and Politics in the Middle East.* London: I. B. Tauris, 1996.

Hammes, Thomas X., *The Sling and the Stone: On war in the 21st Century.* St. Paul, Minn.: Zenith Press, 2004.

Hamud, Randall, ed. *Osama bin Laden: America's Enemy in*

His Own Words. San Diego, Calif.: Nadeem Publishing, 2005.

Heydemann, Steven, ed. *War, Institutions, and Social Change in the Middle East.* Berkeley: University of California Press, 2000.

Hormats, Robert D. *The Price of Liberty: Paying for America's Wars.* NY: Times Books, 2007.

Hourani, Albert. *A History of the Arab People.* Cambridge: Harvard University Press, 1991.

_____. *Arabic Thought in the Liberal Age, 1798-1939.* Cambridge: Cambridge Univ. Press, 1983.

Humphreys, R. Stephen. *Islamic History: A Framework for Inquiry.* Minneapolis: Biblioteca Islamica, 1988.

_____. *Mu'awiya ibn Abu Sufyan: From Arabia To Empire.* Oxford: One World, 2006.

Ibrahim, Raymond. *The Al-Qaeda Reader.* NY: Broadway Books, 2007.

Irving, Washington. *Mahomet and His Successors.* Vol. II. NY: The Continental Press, N.D.

Jackson, Roy. *Fifty Key Figures in Islam.* London: Routledge, 2006. 2006.

Keddie, Nikki. *Religion and Politics in Iran: Shi'ism from Quietism to Revolution.* New Haven, CT: Yale Univ. Press, 1984.

Khalil, Samir. *The Republic of Fear.* NY: Pantheon Books, 1989.

Kramer, Martin. *The Unthinkable Revolution in Iran.* Cambridge: Harvard University Press, 2004.

Krueger, Alan B. *What Makes a Terrorist: Economics and the Roots of Terrorism.* Princeton: Princeton University Press, 2007.

Lawrence, Bruce, ed. *Messages to the World: The Statements of Osama bin Laden.* London: Verso, 2005.

Lawrence, T.E., *The Seven Pillars of Wisdom.* London: Jonathan Cape, 1926.

Lehman, B.H. *Carlyle's Theory of the Hero.* Durham, NC: Duke Univ. Press, 1928.

Lesch, David W. *The Middle East and the United States: A Historical and Political Reassessment.* Boulder, CO.: Westview Press, 1999.

Lewis, Bernard and P.M. Holt, eds. *Historians of the Middle East.* London: OUP, 1962.

Lewis, Bernard. *Islam in History: Ideas, Men and Events in the Middle East.*

London: Alcove. 1973.

_____. *History: Remembered, Recovered, Invented.* Princeton: Princeton Univ. Press, 1975.

_____. ed. *Islam and the ArabWorld.* NY: Alfred A. Knopf, 1976.

_____. *What Went Wrong? Western Impact and Middle Eastern Response.* NY: Oxford University Press, 2002.

_____. *The Crisis of Islam: Holy War and Unholy Terror.* NY: Random House Trade Paperbacks, 2003.

Louis, William Roger. *The British Empire in the Middle East; 1945-1951: Arab Nationalism, the United States, and Postwar Imperialism*. Oxford: Clarendon Press, 1984.

Lowell, Thomas. *With Lawrence in Arabia*. London: Hutchinson, 1994.

Macdonald, D. B. *The Religious Attitudes and Life in Islam*. Beirut: Khayats Publishers, 1965.

Maier, Charles S. *Among Empires: America's Ascendancy and Its Predecessors*.

Cambridge, Mass.: Harvard University Press, 2006.

Malley, Robert. *The Call from Algeria: Third Worldism, Revolution, and the Turn to Islam*. Berkeley: University of California Press, 1996.

Mann, James. *Rise of the Vulcans: The History of Bush's War Cabinet*. NY: Penguin, 2004.

Marx, Karl and Frederick Engels. *On Religion*. Moscow: Progress Publishers, 1985.

McCarthy, Andrew C. *The Grand Jihad: How Islam and the Left Sabotage America*. NY: Encounter Books, 1997.

McDougall, Walter A. *Promised land, Crusader State: The*

American Encounter With the World Since 1776. NY: Houghton Mifflin, 1997.

Mead, Walter Russell. *Power, Terror, Peace, and War: America's Grand Strategy in a World at Risk.* NY: Alfred A. Knopf, 2004.

Meistrich, Ira. "Iraq: The Birthplace of Civilization and War", *Al-Mashriq,* 10, no. 4 (March, 2012), 95-104.

Meyer, Eric. "'I know Thee Not, I Loath Thy Name': Romantic Orientalism in The Eye of the Other", ELH, 58, (1991), 657-699.

Migdal, Joel S. *Strong Societies and Weak States: State-Society Relations and State Capabilities in the Third World.* Princeton, N.J.: Princeton University Press, 1988.

Moussavi, A. K. *Religious Authority in Shi'ite Islam: From the Office of Mufti to The Institution of Marja'.* Kuala Lampur: International Institute of Islamic Thought and Civilization, 1996.

Momen, Moojan. *An Introduction to Shi'i Islam: The*

History and Doctrines of Twelver Shi'ism. New Haven: Yale University press, 1985.

Najmabadeh, Afsaneh. "Iran's Turn to Islam: From Modernism to a Moral Order", *The Middle East Journal.* 41 (1987), 202-17.

Nakash, Yitzhak. *The Shi'is of Iraq.* Princeton: Princeton University Press, 1995.

Nasiri Omar: *Inside the Jihad: My Life With al-Qaeda: A Spy's Story.* NY: Basic Books, 2006.

Nasr, Seyyed Vali. *The Shi'ite Revival: How Conflicts within Islam Will Shape the Future.* NY: W.W. Norton, 2007.

Newman, John Henry, *Historical Sketches.* Vol. I. Westminster, Md.: Christian Classics, 1970.

_____. *The Idea of a University.* New Haven: Yale University Press, 1990.

Nye, Joseph. *Soft Power: The Means to Success in World Politics.* NY: Public Affairs, 2005.

Owen, Roger, and Pamuk, Sevket. *A History of Middle*

East Economics in the Twentieth Century. Cambridge, Mass.: Harvard University Press, 1999.

Patai, Raphael. *The Arab Mind.* NY Scribners, 1973.

Petham, Nicolas. *A New Muslim Order: The Shi'a and the Middle East.* London: I.B. Tauris, 2008.

Richards, Alan, and Waterbury John. *A Political Economy of the Middle East.* Boulder, CO.: Westview Press, 1998.

Robinson, Chase F. *Islamic Historiography.* Cambridge: Cambridge University Press, 2003.

Ruthven, Malise. *Islam in the World.* Oxford: OUP, 2000.

Pape, Robert A. *Dying to Win: The Strategic Logic of Suicide Terrorism.* NY: Random House, 2005.

Phillips, Melanie. *Londonistan.* N.Y.: Encounter Books, 2006.

Reeve, Simon. *The New Jackals: Ramzi Yousef: Osama Bin Laden, and the Future of Terrorism.* Boston: Northeast University Press, 1999.

Richardson, Louise. *What Terrorists Want: Understanding*

the Enemy, Containing the Threat. NY: Random House, 2006.

Sageman, Marc. *Understanding Terror Networks.* Philadelphia, Penn.: University Of Pennsylvania Press, 2004.

Said, Edward W. *Orientalism.* London: Routledge & Kegan Paul, 1978.

Scheuer, Michael F. *Imperial Hubris: Why the West Is Losing the War on Terrorism.* Dulles, Va.: Potomac Books, 2004.

_____. *Marching Toward Hell: America and Islam After Iraq.* NY: Free Press, 2008.

Schwab, Raymond. *The Oriental Renaissance Europe's Rediscovery of India and The East, 1680-1880.* Trans. G. Patterson-Black and V. Reinking. N.Y.: Columbia Univ. Press, 1984.

Shanhan, Rodger. *The Shi'a of Lebanon: Clans, Parties and Clerics.* London: I.B. Tauris, 2005.

Shaw, Harry E. *The Forms of Historical Fiction.* Ithaca Cornell Univ. Press, 1983.

Steyn, Mark. *America Alone: The End of the World as We Know It.* Washington, D.C.: Regnery Publishers, 2006.

Stowasser, Barbara Freyer, ed. *The Islamic Impulse.* Washington, D.C.: Center for Contemporary Arab Studies, 1989.

Trip, Charles. *A History of Iraq.* Cambridge: The Cambridge Univ. Press, 2007.

Tucker, William F. *Mahdis and Millenarians: Shi'ite Extremists in Early Muslim Iraq.* Cambridge: Cambridge Univ. Press, 2008.

Van Creveld, Martin. *The Changing Face of War: Lessons of Combat From the Marne to Iraq.* NY: Ballanyine Books, 2006.

Webster, Alexander F. C., and Darrel Cole. *The Virtue of War: Reclaiming the Classic Traditions East and West.* Salisbury, Mass.: Regina Orthodox Press, 2004.

Wedeen, Lisa. *The Ambiguities of Domination: Politics,*

Rhetoric, and Symbols in Contemporary Syria. Chicago: University of Chicago Press, 1999.

Weigel, George. *The Cube and the Cathedral: Europe, America, and Politics Without God.* NY: Basic Books, 2005.

Wheatcroft, Andrew. *Infidels: A History of the Conflict between Christendom and Islam.* NY: Random House, 2004.

Woodward, Bob. *Bush at War.* NY: Simon and Schuster, 2002.

Ye'or, Bat. *Eurabia: The Euro-Arab Axis.* Madison, N.J.: Farleigh Dickinson University Press, 2005.

Zakaria, Rafiq. *The Struggle Within Islam: The Conflict Between Religion and Politics.* London: Penguin, 1988.

Zubaida, Sami. *Islam, the People, and the State: Political Ideas and Movements in the Middle East.* London: I. B. Tauris, 1993.

Websites

- www.muslim.org/bb/archive/index (Sep. 28.2013).

- wikipedia.org/wiki/Brethren-of-Purity (Sep. 1, 2013).

- en.wikipedia.org/wiki/Ibn_Taymiyyah (July 13, 2013). en.wikipedia.org/wiki/Muslim_Brotherhood (July 12, 2013).

- en.wikipedia.org/wiki/committee-for-the-Promotion-of-Virtue-and-the-Prevention-of-Vice (Sep 5, 2013).

- www.economist.com/node/21547853 (Nov. 13, 2013).

- www.businessweek.com/articles/2012-04-19/the economicvision-of-egypts-muslim-brotherhood-millionaries (Nov. 3, 2013).

Arabic Sources

al-Ajmi, Dhafir Muhammed.

Arabian Gulf Security: Its Development and Problems (amn al-khaleej al-arabi: tatawurhu wa mashalilahu). Beirut: Center for Arab Unity studies. 2006. al-Alawi, Hasan. *American Iraq* (al-iraq al-amreki). London: Zawra' Publishers, 2005.

Faris, Ubeida. "A report on the Conference on Academic Liberties in Iraqi Universities" (taqrir hawl mu'temer al-huriyyat al academia fi al-iraq), *al-Mustaqbal al-Arabi*, no. 327 (April, 2006). 50-76.

Al Da'mi, Muhammed. Islam and Globalization: Arab-Islamic Response to the Outcomes of Globalization (*Al-Islam wa al-awlama: al-Istijaba al-arabiyyah al-islamiyya lemu'tayāt al-awlama*). Abu Dhabi: Emirates Center on Strategic Studies And Reasearch, ecssr, 2003.

_____. Orientalism: The Western Cultural Response to Arab-Islamic History.

(*al-isteshraq: al istehaba al-thaqafia al-gharbuyya liltareekh al-arabi al-islami*). Beirut: Arab Unity Studies center, 2006.

Gharib, Hasan Khalil. *American Organized Crime in Iraq.* Beirut: Darul Tali'a, 2006.

About the author

Muhammed Al Da'mi, M.A., Ph.D. (born, 1955) is Professor of English and Orientalist Literature. His work in the academia exceeds twenty seven years in the universities of Baghdad, Aden, Irbid, Yarmouk and Arizona State. He is author of a number of books and published scholarly papers in Arabic and English. He contributes to the Arabic press weekly. Al Da'mi is a member in several Iraqi and Arabic cultural and specialized societies, including "The House of Wisdom", Baghdad. He has been interviewed by several Arabic and American satellite channels. His books on the Middle East include: *Arabian Mirrors and Western Soothsayers* (2002), *The Other Islam*, revised edition (2013), *Caught in a Dream* (2013) and *The Other Spiritualities of the Middle East* (2013). They all contribute to develop some of the arguments of this book.